*The 4th Michigan
Volunteer Infantry
at Gettysburg*

Michigan State Archives
Unidentified Members of the 4th Michigan

The 4th Michigan Volunteer Infantry at Gettysburg:
The Battle for the Wheatfield

*By
Martin Bertera and
Ken Oberholtzer*

Morningside
1997

Copyright ©1997
by Martin Bertera and Ken Oberholtzer
All rights reserved; no part of this publication may be
reproduced without the written
permission of the Press of Morningside

ISBN: 0-89029-328-7

Morningside House, Inc.
260 Oak Street
Dayton, Ohio 45410
1-800-648-9710
Fax: 937-461-4260

Table of Contents

Acknowledgements ix

Introduction 13

Chapter One
A Brief History of the 4th Michigan Infantry 15

Chapter Two
Onward to Gettysburg 25

Chapter Three
Double Quicking to Gettysburg 53

Chapter Four
The Battle of Gettysburg 59

Chapter Five
The Aftermath 89

Chapter Six
The Pursuit 107

Chapter Seven
In Tribute to the Gallant 4th Michigan 115

Chapter Eight
Michigan Veterans Assistance 120

Appendix One
Gettysburg Casualties of the
4th Michigan Infantry 121

Appendix Two
Roster of the 4th Michigan Infantry 127

Appendix Three
List of Engagements
May 24, 1862, through June 20, 1864 149

Appendix Four
Initial Companies at Unit Muster, June 20, 1861,
Adrian, Michigan 151

Appendix Five
Burial Sites of 4th Michigan Veterans 153

Bibliography 175

Index 181

List of Illustrations

Dwight A. Woodbury 17

John M. Bancroft 28

Rappahannock River, Aerial View 32

Company H, 4th Michigan 35

Rev. John Seage 38

Henry Seage 55

Harrison H. Jeffords 60

Jarius W. Hall 83

Michael J. Vreeland 85

Richard Watson Seage 87

Ebenezer French 93

Benjamin Westfall 98

Surgeon's Certificate of R. Watson Seage 104

Veterans of the 4th Michigan 116

Additional photographs of members of the 4th Michigan appear in the photograph insert at the center of the book.

List of Maps

Third Corps redeploys 66

Fifth Corps deploys 68

Barnes recalls his troops 70

Charge of the 17th Maine 72

Sweitzer changes fronts 79

Sweitzer retreats 81

Acknowledgments

The production of a book is an accomplishment that cannot be achieved single-handedly; the research required, the method in which the research is accomplished, the securing of professional advice and the time needed to convert a mass of data into a story with a logical, historical and sequential flow requires team effort. So it was with this book.

This history would not have been possible without the cooperation and assistance of numerous people; we would like to acknowledge those individuals who were of particular assistance. First we express our sincere thanks to our wives, for their patience and support during the process of research, the hours spent at the keyboard, and the frequent phone calls that took us away from them and our children. Their sacrifice of family time permitted the completion of this book. A heart felt thank you to Debbie Bertera and Marie Oberholtzer and to our children, Jason, Kelly and Aaron Bertera and Mike and Jeff Oberholtzer.

We would also like to express appreciation to our parents, Marshall and Patricia Bertera and Ward and Vivian Oberholtzer, for promoting and supporting the research towards gaining an improved understanding of this era of our American heritage.

We are indebted to two gentlemen who reviewed the manuscript and provided valuable insight and comments. Dr. William Anderson, President of West Shore Community College in Scottville, Michigan, is a Civil War historian, lecturer and author. Brian Pohanka, of Alexandria, Virginia, is a Civil War historian, lecturer, captain of the 5th New York Zouaves and is actively involved with the Association for the Preservation of Civil War Sites (APCWS). Most recently he was an on-site historical advisor to the making of the movie *Gettysburg* based on the novel *The Killer Angels* by Michael Shaara and a contributor and commentator on the Arts & Entertainment's production of *The Civil War Journal*. We offer a sincere thank you to Mr. Pohanka for speaking with Marty Bertera on the movie set of *Gettysburg* in September of 1992 and expressing an interest in reviewing this manuscript before the first key had been depressed on the keyboard. We thank both Dr. Anderson and Mr. Pohanka for their professional critiques and guidance.

The late Judy Mingus of Methuen, Massachusetts, and Dee Seadler of Olney, Maryland, contributed their talents in historical documentation research by providing pension records research of a very specific nature. Their research at the National Archives was thorough, professional and completed in a timely manner. Barbara Steakley and Fran Kirkwood of the Grand Rapids Home For Veterans, formerly The Michigan Soldiers' Home, permitted the review of the Veterans' Home original Burial Book, which provided much information on members of the 4th Michigan who were serviced by that organization since 1886 and which led to the research of admittance records retained in the State Archives. Hazel Monhan of the Hudson Historical Museum and Mrs. Chris Kull of the Monroe Historical Museum provided valuable research assistance for which we are grateful. Dale Niesen graciously provided information and photographs of members of the 4th Michigan. We would also like to thank the following people, who provided valuable research assistance and information: Harriett Anthony, Dr. John T. Daily, Roger Davis, William A. Frassanito, Bessie Boise Haight, Herb E. Hochraldel, Larry Houghton, Roger Hunt, Barbara Krueger, Edgar A. Luce, Jr., Mrs. Joseph McAllister, Mary M. Post, Gene Eric Salecker, Cecile Vreeland, Robert Vreeland, John Heiser and Mac Wyckoff.

Understanding troop movements is always easier when visual aids are available, particularly maps. We would like to express a very special thank you to Mr. Larry Zuidema. Mr. Zuidema is a product design engineer employed by Diesel Technology Company in Grand Rapids, Michigan. He took a hand sketch of the battle area, measuring twenty-six inches by forty-six inches that was not to scale and, using CADRA-III, created the maps that were used as models for the ones that appear in this book. We are grateful for his expertise and participation.

As Civil War re-enactors we have spent hours touring battlefields and gathering around the glow of the campfire to discuss issues, battles and tactics. Space prohibits mentioning the names of all the fellow re-enactors of the 12th South Carolina/4th Michigan Volunteer Infantry. Several of us, however, found ourselves in frequent discussions, and we would like to acknowledge them: Al Coe, Larry Cymbola, Doug Truitt, George Dupuie, Dan Eleson, Dan Flynn, Bill Hanusik, Tom Hout, Craig Maynard, Will Jerden, Brian Benson, Dan Hall, Kevin Johnson, Dick Scott, Bob Minton and the late Bob Helsel.

The research and accumulation of information has spanned six years as we move towards the ultimate objective of a regimental history for the 4th Michigan. We welcome the opportunity to accept further data and correspond with other researchers.

Kenneth H. Oberholtzer							Martin Bertera
Grand Rapids, Michigan							Southgate, Michigan

*Members, 12th South Carolina / 4th Michigan
Volunteer Infantry, Inc.*

Introduction

The 4th Michigan Volunteer Infantry was one of the first Michigan regiments to answer Abraham Lincoln's call for troops in 1861. The 4th Michigan served from June, 1861 through June, 1864 and was subsequently reorganized around a core of 129 veterans into the 4th Michigan Veteran Volunteers under Col. Jarius W. Hall (a second lieutenant of the original 4th Michigan Infantry muster) and sent to serve in the Western Theater. This narrative focuses primarily on the initial enlistment period and particularly on the sixty days between May 25 and July 31, 1863.

As members of the reactivated 4th Michigan Infantry the authors share a common interest in the research and the preservation of the accomplishments and contributions of the 4th Michigan during the War of the Rebellion. The objectives of this narrative are multifaceted. First, we obviously do not wish to glorify war or to suggest that the 4th's contributions were any more or any less important than any other regiment's. It is our aim, however, to honor the men of the 4th and to recognize and pay homage to their efforts and sacrifices. As living historians we commit ourselves to strive to represent, as accurately as possible, the life, the strains, the hardships, the valor and the dedication of the average Civil War soldier. This book is an extension of our commitment. Of supreme importance to living historians is the objective to preserve the history of the American Civil War so that generations to come can better understand and appreciate their national heritage. Most of all, we wish to help preserve the memory of those who bravely fought in the epic struggle.

> Forget not the field where they perished
> the truest, the last of the brave,
>
> All gone—and the bright hope we cherished
> Gone with them, and quenched in their
>   grave![1]

1. John Robertson, ed., *Michigan in the War* (Lansing, Michigan: W. S. George & Company, 1882), p. 220.

Secondly, we wish to introduce the 4th Michigan to the reader. Who were these men? Where did they come from? Where did they contribute their life blood to the Cause? How did they fare during the great struggle? Third, we wish to concentrate on the regiment's activities during the thirty days before and after the battle of Gettysburg with specific emphasis on the 4th's role in the Wheatfield.

The research for this book has been extensive. Like any research, it is never complete but merely a snapshot in time. Our intent is not to question history, nor to question authoritative interpretations of events. Our objective is to accumulate data specific to the 4th Michigan so that its role in history can be more clearly understood and presented to the casual reader.

We now invite you to sit back and enjoy *The 4th Michigan At Gettysburg*.

Chapter One
A Brief History of the 4th Michigan Volunteer Infantry

The hour was sad I left the maid,
   a lingering farewell taking
Her sighs and tears my steps delay'd,
   I thought her heart was breaking;
In hurried words her name I bless'd,
   I breathed the vows that bind me,
And to my heart in anguish press'd
   the girl I left behind me.

"The Blow At Last Fallen. WAR! WAR! WAR! The Confederate Batteries Open On Sumter Yesterday Morning"
Detroit Free Press, April 13, 1861

General Order No. 17:
   The following appointments are hereby made in the Michigan troops:
     Dwight A. Woodbury, Colonel 4th Regiment
     William W. Duffield, Lt. Colonel 4th Regiment
     Jonathan W. Childs, Major 4th Regiment.
   The 4th Regiment will be rendezvoused at Adrian as soon as quarters are ready. The field officers of the 4th will report by letter to Colonel Woodbury at Adrian forthwith. By order of the Commander-in-chief.

                            Jno. Robertson
                            Adjutant General
                            Detroit, Michigan
                            May 16, 1861[1]

   In 1861, Michigan, like other states, was undoubtedly preparing for the worse case scenario: war. Col. Dwight A. Woodbury held his commission in the Michigan militia and was prominent

---

1. Robertson, *Michigan in the War*, p. 222.

in state military affairs. Because of Colonel Woodbury's prominence, the 4th Michigan was one of the first Michigan regiments mustered into three year service.

Recruiting had been underway for an undisclosed period of time. General Order Number 24, issued on May 20, 1861, by Jonathan Robertson, Michigan's Adjutant General, identified the ten companies and their officers.[2] What was unusual about the command structure was that Company I had two captains, at least on paper. David A. Granger was commissioned captain on May 16 and mustered in on June 20, 1861, in accordance with General Order Number 24. Some time between June 20 and 30, David Granger resigned and left for Massachusetts, where, on September 20, 1861, he enlisted in Company C of the 11th Massachusetts Infantry as a first lieutenant. He would regain a captaincy by September 15, 1863. Jeremiah D. Slocum originally enlisted in Company B as first lieutenant and was commissioned on May 16. Upon Captain Granger's resignation, Slocum was promoted to captain of Company I and commissioned on June 20, 1861. A review of the 4th Michigan Infantry enlistment rolls also reveal some rather interesting statistics about ages and demographics.[3]

The majority of the 4th Michigan Infantry came from the state's southeastern counties; however, the 4th also drew soldiers from neighboring states, Virginia, and Canada as well. Indiana contributed thirty-five soldiers divided nearly evenly between Steuben and LaGrange counties, both of which border Michigan. Ohio contributed sixteen soldiers, although these enlistments appear to be random as the soldiers came from numerous counties. One soldier came from Illinois and one from Virginia. Joseph Burce of Fairfax, Virginia, enlisted in Company B on June 20. Wounded at Gettysburg, Burce served with the 4th Michigan throughout the war, after which he returned to Virginia. Canada contributed seven soldiers. Two of the seven, John Miller of Montreal and George Parker of Frankfort, were substitutes for draftees. Both men enlisted in Company K in March 1863 and were absent without leave within thirty days en route to Washington. John Mooney enlisted in Company I in June 1861 but had skipped off by the end of July 1861.[4] Yet Canada sent good, brave, honorable men as

---

2. Robertson, *Michigan in the War*, p. 222. A chart of the original ten companies appears in Appendix Four.
3. G. H. Brown, *Record Fourth Michigan Infantry: Civil War, 1861-1865* (Detroit: Detroit Book Press, n.d.), p. 222.
4. "Skipped off" was a term used to describe the incidence when a soldier deserted.

Hudson Historical Museum

Dwight A. Woodbury

Dwight A. Woodbury of Adrian, Michigan, was a thirty-six-year-old colonel in the state militia at the outbreak of hostilities. He received his commission as colonel on May 16, 1861, and was mustered in at Adrian on June 20, 1861. Colonel Woodbury was killed by a gunshot wound to the head while leading his men on July 1, 1862, at the battle of Malvern Hill. He is buried in Adrian.

well. George Blankman of Quebec joined Company K and was eventually listed as missing in action. Richard Martin of Montreal joined Company I in June 1861, and was discharged on disability in January 1862. Andrew Forbes of Woodstock, Canada, joined Company I on June 20, 1861. He was discharged one year later as "a minor and British subject." Charles L. Schutze from Sandwich, Canada, joined Company I on June 20, 1861, and was killed in action at Malvern Hill on July 1, 1862.[5]

As far as age distribution went, the 4th Michigan was not a teenage army. The average age was twenty-three years, seven months. The average age of the initial compliment of officers was thirty-one years, seven months. The range of ages was quite extraordinary, from fourteen to sixty-one. Twenty-three percent were under nineteen, fifty-five percent were between twenty and twenty-five, eleven percent were between twenty-six and thirty, nine percent were in their thirties and two percent were over forty.[6]

The two youngest soldiers were fourteen and sixteen; both were musicians. Their instruments were most likely drums since drummers served multiple purposes. In camp such musicians played various commands, while on the march they kept the beat for marching soldiers, and while on the field of battle they could beat field commands as ordered by the commanding officer including firing by drum. Henry A. Leming was fourteen when he enlisted in Wayne County in Company I on June 20, 1861. Young Henry served with the 4th Michigan for twenty-one months before he was discharged due to disability on March 16, 1863. LeRoy M. Spencer was sixteen when he enlisted in Company K at Flowerfield, Michigan, on September 18, 1862. Spencer served the balance of the war and was discharged on June 5, 1865.[7]

On the other end of the age spectrum were two men who tried to contribute to the Union cause. Eli Burke, from Hillsdale County, was sixty-one when he enlisted on June 20, 1861, as a musician. A man of his age, however, apparently could not withstand the rigors of camp and army life as he was discharged on disability on August 13 after two months of service. Noah Cressey of Lenawee County was fifty-two when he enlisted in Company F on June 20, 1861, as a musician. He was discharged on disability thirteen months later on July 20, 1862.[8]

5. Brown, *Record Fourth Michigan*, pp. 15, 20, 43, 75-78, 84, 97.
6. *Ibid.*, pp. 4-127.
7. *Ibid.*, pp. 68, 103.
8. *Ibid.*, pp. 21, 31.

The 4th Michigan rendezvoused at Camp Williams in Adrian, Michigan. Camp Williams was the campus of Adrian College with the north wing acting as "capital dormitories for the men" as recorded in a local newspaper on May 28. The same article describes a typical day at Camp Williams. "An informal daily routine has already been established, as follows: reveille at 5 a.m.; breakfast at 6:30; squad drill from 9 to 11; dinner at 12:30 p.m.; company drill from 2 to 5; supper at 6; tattoo at 9:30; taps at 10." This schedule remained intact until the regiment was mustered into service on June 20. Of particular interest is the type of uniform initially provided to the soldiers as reported in the *Adrian Expositor*. "The Third and Fourth Regiments are to be uniformed with gray cloth, which in many respects is preferable to blue, not as soon showing the effects of age and not being so liable to fade. Tents have also been contracted for and will soon be completed."[9]

In a public ceremony on June 21, the 4th Michigan received its regimental colors from the women of Adrian as presented by Mrs. W. S. Wilcox. The regiment formed a hollow square formation so that all troops could hear the various speakers, including Mrs. Wilcox, Colonel Woodbury, C. M. Croswell, Esquire and the Honorable Zachariah Chandler. Colonel Woodbury accepted the regimental flag with a speech that demonstrated the loyalty that typically is seen throughout accounts of battle heroics: "In whatever position we may be assigned, with our banner to cheer us, we will strive to do our duty as American soldiers. To no inferior force shall it ever be surrendered, and sooner than be trailed to treason it shall become the pall of the regiment."[10]

> With rolling drum and banners gay,
> We sent them from our arms away;
> With kisses on their lips yet warm
> They met the battle's fearful storm[11]

The 4th Michigan Infantry remained at Adrian for four more days, departing for Washington by rail on June 25 at 11 a.m. with a compliment of 37 officers and 988 men for a total of 1,025 soldiers. They were led by their eighteen member regimental band under the direction of twenty-five-year-old Drum Major Isaac Diffenbaugh. The 4th's band was recruited from

---

9. *Adrian Expositor*, May 28, 1861, Adrian Public Library, Adrian, Michigan.
10. *Michigan in the War*, p. 223.
11. *Ibid.*, p. 291.

Cleveland, Ohio, where it had been under the leadership of John Von Olker. In addition to the eighteen member band, there were eighteen musicians assigned to the various companies. Also included in the procession was one chaplain, three medical staff personnel and eight wagoners. Total enrollment, then, on June 25, 1861, was 1,050 volunteers.[12]

The regiment marched to the train station where they boarded "25 coaches and a number of baggage and freight cars" furnished by the Cleveland & Erie Railroad. The procession passed through Toledo, Ohio, on June 25 and arrived in Cleveland at 7 p.m.[13] The unarmed regiment continued its journey by rail to Harrisburg, Pennsylvania, where the men received their armament. Michigan, in general, seems to have sent her sons to war well equipped; a civic leader of Cleveland, Ohio, described the Michigan troops as "splendidly armed and equipped." A correspondent in Harrisburg exclaimed, "Has Michigan sent another regiment equipped?"[14]

The 4th Michigan reached Washington during the night of July 2, and took up position with the 2nd and 3rd Michigan Infantry near the "chain bridge" above Georgetown. The regiment was used largely to help construct the defenses around Washington City including Fort Woodbury, located in Arlington, Virginia.[15]

Few men of the 4th Michigan could envision what truly lay ahead when they gathered at Camp Williams on the grounds of Adrian College during May and June of 1861. For many, joining the 4th represented opportunities for adventure, anticipated heroism, honor, preservation of the Union, abolition of slavery or perhaps merely a chance to leave their communities or farmlands to travel to other parts of the country. It is hard to conceive that they knew what hardships lay ahead. It would not be long before the 4th Michigan would begin experiencing the harshness of Civil War military life.

By August 4, Gen. George B. McClellan had finished the first phase of his organization of the Division of the Potomac, as the Army of the Potomac was initially called. The 4th Michigan was assigned to Brig. Gen. William T. Sherman's brigade, which included the 9th and 14th Massachusetts, the 41st New

---

12. Brown, *Record Fourth Michigan.*
13. *Toledo Blade,* June 25, 1861, Toledo Public Library, Toledo, Ohio; *Cleveland Plain Dealer,* June 25, 1861, Cleveland Public Library, Cleveland, Ohio; *Cleveland Plain Dealer,* June 26, 1861.
14. Robertson, *Michigan in the War,* p. 223.
15. *Ibid.,* p. 224. Fort Woodbury was named for Colonel Woodbury.

York, Hamilton's Battery E of the 2nd U.S. Artillery and Company I of the 2nd U.S. Cavalry.[16]

The 4th Michigan remained in Sherman's brigade until McClellan completed his next organizational phase on October 15. The Division of the Potomac had been transformed into the Army of the Potomac. The former brigade structure had now been expanded to the larger division structure comprised of infantry with cavalry and artillery batteries attached. The 4th Michigan was assigned to Brig. Gen. Fitz-John Porter's division. It was attached to Brig. Gen. George W. Morell's brigade along with the 33rd Pennsylvania, 9th Massachusetts and the 4th New York.[17]

The regiment went into winter quarters at Miner's Hill, Virginia, and in the early spring was assigned to Morell's Second Brigade of Porter's First Division of Brig. Gen. Samuel P. Heintzelman's Third Corps.[18] By May 18, 1862, the Fifth Corps was created and the 4th Michigan reassigned to Brig. Gen. Charles Griffin's Second Brigade of Morell's First Division of Porter's Fifth Corps for McClellan's Peninsular Campaign. The 4th Michigan was sent to the siege of Yorktown where its first officer casualty of war was Capt. Abram R. Wood, ironically, of Company C, the Peninsular Guard. Captain Wood, who was thirty-five years old, was killed while on picket duty.[19]

The regiment's first significant engagement came on May 24, at Newbridge, Virginia. From that day until June 18, 1864, the 4th Michigan Volunteer Infantry saw continuous action.[20]

> Forward to battle for God and the right!
> Hurrah for the banner!
> Hurrah for the banner!
> Hurrah for the banner, the flag of the free![21]

Civil War statistics indicate that for every man killed in action, two more died of disease. The 4th Michigan did not fit this pattern. On the contrary, for every two soldiers who were

---

16. United States War Department, *The War of the Rebellion: A Compilation of the Official Records of the Union and Confederate Armies*, 70 vols., 128 parts (Washington, D.C.: Government Printing Office, 1880-1901), series 1, vol. 5, p. 15. (Hereafter cited as *OR*. All subsequent references are to Series 1 unless otherwise noted.)
17. *Ibid.*, pp. 15, 16.
18. Robertson, *Michigan in the War*, p. 224; *OR*, vol. 5, pt. 1, pp. 19, 20.
19. Frederick C. Dyer, *Compendium of the War of the Rebellion* (Des Moines, Iowa: Dyer, 1908), p. 1283; Brown, *Record Fourth Michigan*, pp. 3, 4, 124.
20. See the List of Engagements in Appendix Three.
21. Robertson, *Michigan in the War*, p. 705.

killed in action, died of wounds, or died as prisoners of war, only one soldier died as the result of disease. In the final analysis, the war took an appalling toll on the 4th Michigan Infantry. Of the 1,399 soldiers enrolled, over 49 percent of them—or 692 men—were lost to the regiment either through death or disability discharge.[22]

As can be expected, officers who actively led their men rather than pushed them suffered high casualty rates. Of the original compliment of officers, eight died during or following battles: Abram R. Wood at Yorktown; Richard B. DePuy, Simon B. Preston, and Jeptha Beers at Gaines' Mill; A. Morell Rose and Dwight A. Woodbury at Malvern Hill; Harrison H. Jeffords at Gettysburg; and George Lumbard at the Wilderness. Another seven officers resigned on disability.[23]

Colonel Woodbury experienced a close call at Newbridge, Virginia, near the Chickahominy River on May 24, as attested by a Rebel prisoner. "I might have shot you half a dozen times" said the prisoner. "Why didn't you?" asked the Colonel, coolly. "I took you for some damned common orderly!" was the reply.[24] Colonel Woodbury's good fortune would continue until July 1, at Malvern Hill:

> The enemy in full force still pressed them hard, determined at one fell swoop to utterly destroy and capture all that remained of that proud army. Late in the afternoon fresh rebel troops were massed, and, confident of success, were hurled upon our jaded, wearied men. With death-defying determination three times they charged.... There, in full dress, cool and collected, passing from rank to rank, "mid death shots falling thick and fast, as lightnings from the mountain cloud," was Woodbury. It is said there was an unusual sadness in the expression on his face as he went into that battle, as though he had a premonition that his time had come; yet steadily he went forward as to a holiday parade. On the very eve of victory, when animating his men and gallantly cheering them on, a rebel bullet pierced his brain and stilled as brave a heart as ever throbbed. "On, my brave boys, on" and "good bye, boys" were the last words that passed from his lips.[25]

22. Brown, *Record Fourth Michigan*, p. 3.
23. *Ibid.*, pp. 12, 35, 61, 71, 90, 95, 124, 125.
24. Robertson, *Michigan in the War*, p. 224
25. *Ibid.*, p. 226

The 4th's respected leader and first commander was dead.

The quotation is a good example of the way in which writers of the time often romanticized the war and spoke eloquently—yet abstractly—of bravery. So called "last words" sometimes must be read with the author's creative license in mind, particularly in light of the soldier's wound; in this case Col. Woodbury was to have uttered his last words with a fatal head wound. Capt. John M. Randolph reported "Colonel Woodbury was everywhere present, and by his example and courage inspired every one with renewed vigor. About half an hour after the action commenced he was mortally wounded, the ball penetrating the head just above the right eye. While being borne from the field his last words were: 'good bye, boys.'"[26] Surg. David P. Chamberlain reported:

> our regiment occupied the extreme left of the line of battle at "Malvern Hill." Towards evening a regiment of our brigade was ordered to charge on the advancing rebels; but after advancing halfway across the field the fire was so severe they were compelled to break and fall back in great confusion, passing through the 4th Michigan regiment, who were lying on their faces to escape the fire of the enemy. Colonel Woodbury was at the head of the regiment, and Captain [A. Morell] Rose, of Monroe, [Company A] and Captain [Marshall W.] Chapin, of Company F, were near by in charge of their companies. The Colonel attempted to rally the retreating regiment, shouting to them with his cap in one hand and his sword in the other, telling them to stand their grounds, that they and the 4th could check the enemy. At this moment he was pierced in the forehead by a musket ball. He threw up his arms and fell back dead. His countenance in death appeared calm but earnest. His under lip was clasped under his upper teeth, a habit of his life, indicating his earnestness of purpose.[27]

Following Colonel Woodbury's death, Lt. Col. Jonathan W. Childs was promoted to colonel and commanded the regiment until his resignation on November 25, 1862. Command then temporarily passed to Lt. Col. George Lumbard.[28]

---

26. *Ibid.*, p. 227.
27. *Ibid.*
28. Brown, *Record Fourth Michigan*, pp. 25, 71.

With his back to the field and his feet to the
   foe!
And leaving in battle no blot on his name,
Looks proudly to Heaven from the deathbed of
   fame.
He had fought his last battle,
No sound shall awake him to glory again.[29]

  The 4th Michigan was under the command of at least four colonels during its three year term: Dwight Woodbury, Jonathan Childs, Harrison Jeffords and George Lumbard. Lt. Col. Jarius W. Hall appears to have been in command between May 7 and June 19, 1864, when the regiment left Petersburg via City Point bound for Washington. Lieutenant Colonel Hall went on to be the colonel of the Reorganized 4th Michigan Veteran Volunteers. Colonel Woodbury would not be the only leader to die in battle while leading the 4th; another would be lost in the Wheatfield.[30]

---

29. Robertson, *Michigan in the War*, p. 226.
30. Brown, *Record Fourth Michigan*, pp. 25, 51, 61, 71, 125.

Chapter Two
Onward to Gettysburg

Tracing the march of the 4th Michigan into the annals of history and its contributions at Gettysburg begins on Monday May 25, 1863. The weather was exceedingly warm but not unlike the preceding days. The 4th Michigan was in Maj. Gen. George G. Meade's Fifth Corps, Brig. Gen. James Barnes' First Division, and Col. Jacob Sweitzer's Second Brigade. General Barnes of Massachusetts was in command of the First Division, replacing General Griffin, who had been temporarily relieved due to ill health and reassigned to command Harpers Ferry. General Barnes and Colonel Sweitzer, though accomplished military commanders, were relatively new to their current commands. Col. Harrison H. Jeffords was in command of the 4th.[1]

Sixty-one-year-old Barnes, a West Point graduate, entered the service as colonel of the 18th Massachusetts. He commanded the First Brigade at Antietam, Fredericksburg and Chancellorsville. When Griffin was reassigned, Barnes was promoted to the command of the First Division.[2]

Jacob Bowman Sweitzer was a lawyer from Pittsburgh when he enlisted as a major of the 62nd Pennsylvania Infantry. He was promoted to colonel of the regiment in 1862. Colonel Sweitzer rose to the command of the Second Brigade prior to the battle of Fredericksburg.[3]

Harrison H. Jeffords was the twenty-four-year-old son of Solomon and Phebe Jeffords of Dexter, Michigan. The Jeffords family operated a brick farm on the outskirts of Dexter between the villages of Dexter and Lima in Lima Township. Harrison

---

1. *OR*, vol. 27, p. 161; *Hillsdale Standard*, June 30, 1863, Mitchell Public Library, Hillsdale, Michigan; *OR*, vol. 25, p. 163. The battle of Chancellorsville preceded Gettysburg. General Griffin was in command of the First Division and Col. James McQuade was in command of the Second Brigade. *OR*, vol. 25, p. 516.
2. Mark Boatner, *The Civil War Dictionary* (New York: McKay, 1959), p. 45.
3. *Ibid.*, p. 823; Harry W. Pfanz, *Gettysburg: The Second Day* (Chapel Hill: University of North Carolina Press, 1987), pp. 243-44.

Jeffords was the oldest of six children. Jeffords had attended the University of Michigan Law School in Ann Arbor, where he received his law degree with the school's second graduating class of forty-four. The young lawyer took up residence in Dexter, some twenty miles west of Ann Arbor, and practiced law in Lima, Dexter and Ann Arbor. In December, 1857 Solomon Jeffords transferred sixty-seven acres of the brick farm to Harrison, his oldest child.[4]

At the outbreak of the hostilities between the states, Jeffords enlisted in Company K as a first lieutenant receiving his commission on May 16, 1861, and being mustered into service at Camp Williams in Adrian on June 20. Before leaving the state the dutiful lawyer made a will which granted to his mother the "Brick Yard lot," essentially the entire farm.[5] His military potential was recognized and his star began to rise. By May 1, 1862, he was commissioned as captain of Company C. On March 13, 1863, he was commissioned colonel of the 4th, retroactive to November 26, 1862, replacing Lt. Col. George Lumbard who had been in temporary command of the regiment.[6]

Early in 1863 Captain Jeffords, serving as acting major, determined that the ranks of the 4th required replenishment. On February 1 he requested a fifteen day leave, commencing on the 28th to travel to Michigan to recruit new troops.[7] The leave was granted and he left for Michigan. Captain Jeffords, however, had objectives far beyond that of securing new troops. Upon his arrival in Detroit, he reported to Lieutenant Colonel Smith of the Provost Guard. During his leave he was actively involved in recruiting. In addition, he had gained an audience with Gov. Austin Blair to seek approval of field promotions and to seek his own promotion. While in Michigan he overstayed his leave by forty-eight hours. He returned to the regiment on March 16 as its new colonel, surprising everyone, particularly Lieutenant Colonel Lumbard who had been acting colonel since November 15, 1862. Upon arrival to the regiment he made a written report to the brigade commander explaining the delay in his return.[8]

Shortly after Jeffords returned to the regiment, he was ordered to appear before a Court Martial Commission to answer

4. B. Krueger, "Information Involving Harrison H. Jeffords," (Research Paper, Eastern Michigan University, 1992), pp. 1-2.
5. *Ibid.*
6. Brown, *Record Fourth Michigan*, p. 61, 71.
7. Harrison H. Jeffords to "Asst. Adjt. Gen.," February 1, 1863, Michigan State Archives, Lansing, Michigan.
8. John Bancroft to T. J. Hinchman, February 8, 1863, Burton Collection.

to charges of being absent without leave. These charges appear to have been brought by Lumbard in an effort to retain his own leadership position. Jeffords' absence, however, had been under the orders of Lieutenant Colonel Smith who had requested that he take charge of the new recruits and deliver them to the various Michigan units. Consequently, on March 18 Colonel Jeffords wrote a letter to Smith reciting the problem and requesting written confirmation of the situation. The letter read in part:

> Immediately on my return I made an explanation in writing to Comdr of the Brigade stating that I reported to you before the expiration of my "leave of absence" (which was the case) and that you ordered me to report at a subsequent period to take charge of a Detachment of men for different Mich Regiments....You will greatly oblige me by giving the subject your attention and send me as good a defense as possible.[9]

Court martial charges were soon dropped. However, stress in the command structure must surely have existed, since Jeffords had left as a captain and returned as a colonel, displacing one who had been in command for at least three months.

Jeffords' political savvy and influence are quite evident, but was he respected by those whom he commanded? The answer appears to be an unequivocal yes as recorded by Lt. John Bancroft: "Colonel Jeffords has arrived and was treated with a public gathering. A thing very unusual here. He spoke a few words which were well received by the men who proposed three cheers for Col. Jeffords. The men and most of the officers are well pleased." On April 10 he wrote, "Col. Jeffords has been court martialed for being away beyond his leave of absence. We all hope he will soon be in command of the regiment for the Lt. Col. [Lumbard] has lost rather than gained for his action since Jeffords promotion. On Brigade drill he has showed his ignorance of tactics and he is quite irritable generally."[10] Perhaps a more visible demonstration of the extent to which he was held in esteem by his troops occurred during company parade on April 11, 1863, as recorded by Cpl. Henry Seage: "At parade the

---

9. Harrison H. Jeffords to Lieutenant Colonel Smith, May 18, 1863, Heckert Collection; Harrison Jeffords to T. J. Hinchman, April 10, 1863, Burton Collection.
10. John Bancroft to T. H. Hinchman, March 16, 1863, Burton Collection, Detroit Public Library, Detroit, Michigan; John Bancroft to T. H. Hinchman, April 10, 1863, Burton Collection.

Dearborn Historical Museum

John M. Bancroft

John M. Bancroft, of Wayne County, was mustered into service in Adrian on June 20, 1861, as sergeant of Company I at the age of eighteen. He rose through the ranks receiving promotions to first sergeant, second lieutenant of Company C, first lieutenant of Company K, first lieutenant of Company H and first lieutenant of Company B. He was mustered out in Detroit on June 30, 1864, at the expiration of his enlistment.

regiment presented Colonel Jeffords with a fine horse fully equipped." The magnificent gift was presented by Sgt. Maj. R. Watson Seage.[11]

Following the battle of Chancellorsville, the Fifth Corps was encamped near Falmouth, Virginia, across the Rappahannock from Fredericksburg. Edward Taylor wrote that "everyone is obliged to wear his badge" visually signifying the corps to which each soldier belonged. The headquarters flag of the Fifth Corps was a "white square flag with a large red maltese cross."[12] It can be assumed that most troops were busying themselves by making and affixing their badges to their caps and jackets. The Chancellorsville battle had been fierce, and afterwards the men of the 4th could scarcely believe their good fortune to draw picket duty, along with the Fifth Corps, guarding the railroads and roads from Potomac Creek to Falmouth.[13] The land near Stoneman's Switch upon which the 4th was camped had been used previously; consequently, the area was as one soldier described it, "dreary and desolate without trees or green fields for miles." To compound the dreariness, most of the available wood had been consumed during the previous encampment.[14]

On Tuesday May 26 word came to the 4th Michigan that Gov. Austin Blair was visiting the Michigan regiments and was expected to visit the 4th on the 27th. On Wednesday, May 27, not only did Governor Blair arrive but he brought along his wife, a niece and another lady, a pleasant sight indeed for battle-weary soldiers. In addition, the paymaster had arrived as well. Governor Blair reviewed the brigade at one o'clock in the afternoon. Immediately following the review the brigade formed a hollow square so that all could more easily hear his speech which included the presentation of a new regimental flag. The Governor ended his visit leaving the camp by 7 p.m.[15]

The men of the 4th had reason to be proud. After Chancellorsville, their flag, a source of great regimental pride, "was so torn and cut from shot and shell that it could not be

11. Henry Seage journal, April 11, 1863, Steve Roberts Collection, Northville, Michigan.
12. Edward Taylor to Lottie, May 21, 1863, Michigan Historical Collection.
13. George Lumbard, letter dated May 25, 1863, appearing in the *Hillsdale Standard*, July 2, 1863.
14. *Monroe Commercial*, June 2, 1863, Monroe County Library, Monroe, Michigan.
15. *Monroe Commercial*, June 2, 1863; Jim Houghton journal, May 27, 1863, Michigan Historical Collection, University of Michigan, Ann Arbor, Michigan; John Bancroft journal, May 27, 1863, Michigan Historical Collection; Seage journal, May 27, 1863.

carried."[16] The flag was retired and replaced with a new one. Colonel Jeffords saw fit to return the old one to the ladies of Adrian, who had originally presented it, for safe keeping. It thus became a source of pride for all of Michigan and not just the men of the 4th who carried it through so many battles. The 4th now had a new flag and an opportunity to carry on the tradition signified by their last one.[17]

Thursday morning May 28, 1863, began much like any other day in camp. There were camp chores to do, letters home to write and military paperwork to complete, such as Colonel Jefford's letter to Governor Blair advising him of field commissions and seeking his approval. On May 28, 1863, Colonel Jeffords requested the following promotions:

> Captain Jarius Hall to major from May 22, 1863
> Sergeant Major R. Watson Seage to Second Lieutenant from April 1, 1863
> Sergeant George W. Bradford to Second Lieutenant from September 13, 1862.[18]

The day held two special events for the men of the 4th. First, it was payday and most men received two months pay in the morning. The second event is obvious only in retrospect, for this day marked the beginning of the long journey to Gettysburg and immortality in the annals of history.[19]

In the afternoon of May 28 the Fifth Corps received orders to march to Kelly's Ford on the upper Rappahannock River which is located approximately twenty-five miles above Fredericksburg, Virginia; Kelly's Ford was deep, swift and 300 feet wide.[20] By 5 or 6 p.m. the tents were struck and the 4th was on the march, heading towards Hartwood Church some eight miles northwest of Falmouth on the Warrenton Post Road arriving there at nine in the evening. Sometime after one in the morning, the 4th was on the march again guided by a "bright full moon and a cool breeze."[21] They marched fifteen miles to

16. Edward Taylor to Lottie, May 21, 1863, Michigan Historical Collection.
17. Robert Campbell, "Pioneer Memories of the War Days 1861-1865," *Historical Collections: Collections and Researches Made by the Michigan Pioneer and Historical Society*, Vol. 30 (Lansing, Michigan: Wyncop, Hallenbeck, Crawford Co., 1906), p. 567.
18. Harrison H. Jeffords to Gov. Austin Blair, May 18, 1863, Michigan State Archives.
19. Houghton journal, May 28, 1863; Bancroft journal, May 28, 1863; *Monroe Commerical*, June 2, 1863.
20. *Hillsdale Standard*, June 30, 1863.
21. Francis J. Parker, *The Story of the Thirty-second Regiment Massachusetts Infantry* (Boston: Calkins, 1880), p. 159.

Kelly's Ford during a day that had grown progressively warmer and arrived at 2 p.m. and pitched tents in what one soldier described as a "good camp" with "plenty of shade and green fields." The Second Brigade was ordered to guard Kelly's Ford and the adjacent ones. Consequently, upon their arrival the Second Brigade was divided with the 32nd and 9th Massachusetts regiments continuing to Ellis's Ford, now called Barnett's Ford, a few miles downriver. The 62nd Pennsylvania and 4th Michigan stayed at Kelly's Ford. By late afternoon the 4th was on picket duty along the north bank facing Rebel pickets.[22]

The warm Virginian spring continued through Saturday. By Sunday, May 31, the heat subsided yielding a "very pleasant," "cool and breezy" day. The 4th was on picket duty all day so Chaplain John Seage did not have the opportunity to provide a "divine service" for the boys. There was apparently, however, some free time created by alternating active picket duty between companies. Individual free time was used for a host of purposes; writing letters, cooking meals, and cleaning weapons for the almost daily late afternoon inspections. But considering the marches of late, the continually warm weather and their current location, the men of the 4th did the obvious thing as Corporal Seage related, "almost all of the company [E] went fishing and swimming."[23]

Henry S. Seage was one of three men from the Seage family who served in the Union army. Henry joined his brother, Richard Watson, in Company E of the 4th. Later their father, John, would join them. Henry enlisted on September 27, 1861, in the village of Hudson and was mustered into service on October 8, 1861. Henry, holding the rank of corporal, was mustered out on September 10, 1864, in Petersburg, Virginia, after completing his term of service.[24]

The month of June was ushered in with a continuation of Sunday's cool temperatures. The day found the 4th maintaining the routine of picket duty and 5 p.m. inspections. Lt. Michael Vreeland used his personal time to buy some handmade gingham cloth from a local young lady who boasted of making the cloth from the raw material. While Lieutenant Vreeland was negotiating with the local fabric maker, other soldiers were appreciatively taking in the sights of the other young ladies that graced the Kelly's Ford locale. As Lieutenant Bancroft wrote, "Young ladies are quite good looking. Sesesh

22. *Monroe Commercial*, June 2, 1863; Bancroft journal, May 29, 1863.
23. Bancroft journal, May 31, 1863; Seage journal, May 31, 1863.
24. Brown, *Record Fourth Michigan*, p. 98.

John T. Dailey Collection

Rappahannock River

This aerial photograph of the Rappahannock River was taken in 1986. Kelly's Ford is located at the foot of the island below the bridge.

too. Very bad." June 1 was an important day for Edward H. Taylor of Company B who was promoted to sergeant major.[25]

Michael J. Vreeland of Brownstown, Michigan, was twenty-two years old when he was mustered into service at Camp Williams in Adrian, Michigan, on June 20, 1861, as sergeant of Company I. His younger cousin, nineteen-year-old William J. Vreeland accompanied him but was discharged on a surgeon's certificate just forty days later, July 30. Michael Vreeland had an illustrious military career. His leadership capabilities were quickly acknowledged with a promotion to first sergeant by January 13, 1862. Seven months later he received a commission as second lieutenant; a first lieutenant promotion came just forty-five days later on October 16, 1862. Vreeland held this commission until his discharge on June 30, 1864. His civilian days lasted but a mere two and one half months. The Reorganized 4th Michigan was formed around a core of 129 veterans, one of which was Capt. Michael Vreeland. His captain's rank was replaced with a commission to lieutenant colonel. His rise continued to that of brevet colonel and brigadier general of U.S. Volunteers on March 13, 1865. General Michael Vreeland was mustered out on May 26, 1866, in Houston, Texas.[26]

John M. Bancroft was eighteen when he was mustered into Company I as sergeant on June 20, 1861, in Adrian. He rose to first sergeant by July 1, 1862, then quickly to second lieutenant of Company C in the same month. First lieutenant bars were awarded on September 3, 1862, providing leadership to Company K then Company H by March 12, 1863. Bancroft served until being mustered out on June 30, 1864, having completed his term of service.[27]

Tuesday, June 2, was not much different from the previous days as picket duty continued along the river and in rifle pits followed by late afternoon inspection. The day was warmer, enticing the men of the 4th back into the river for a swim. The men on the other side of the river also heard the call of the cool, refreshing river as Corporal Seage related: "a lot of us went in swimming, Rebs on their side." The day ended uneventfully with a light rain in the night.[28]

25. Seage journal, June 1, 1863; Bancroft journal, June 1, 1863; Brown, *Record Fourth Michigan*, p. 108. "Sesesh" was the term occassionally used to refer to a member of the Southern populace. It is short for secessionist.
26. Brown, *Record Fourth Michigan*, p. 115.
27. *Ibid.*, p. 9.
28. Seage journal, June 2, 1863.

Thursday, June 4 was a very warm day. Camp life continued with picket duty and daily inspections. The men of the 4th had been together for almost two years and presumably grown to trust and rely on one another. However, trust can be both elusive and easily misplaced as Pvt. Jim Houghton's comment suggests: "Today I got 37 dollars of my money stole." Thursday blended with Friday and the days became one as camp life continued and the day ended with a 5 p.m. inspection.[29]

The Confederate forces were on the opposite bank of the Rappahannock River. From observation balloon reports, reports from interrogation of Confederate deserters and cavalry reports there appears to have been much apprehension as to when and where the Rebels would cross the river. Maj. Gen. Joseph Hooker issued a general order on June 5 that reflected his concern. It read, in part, "this army will be held in readiness. . . . Three days' cooked rations will be kept on hand until further orders."[30]

Saturday, June 6 brought picket duty on the Rappahannock River. This day the boys received orders to be prepared to march with three days rations but nothing developed from the alert. While on picket duty, Lieutenant Bancroft noted the scenic beauty of the area: "fine view . . . open fields . . . hills of the Blue Ridge in the distance . . . valley of the Rappahannock . . . roses, laurel blossoms and pure air." These words paint a picture of natural beauty unencumbered by modern day "civilized improvements." Bancroft continued describing the Rappahannock River as "very rocky" with "rapids and dams" and "bluffs in places."[31]

Picket duty could serve more than merely guarding one's flank and talking between opposing pickets could be more than idle talk as Maj. Gen. Daniel Butterfield's June 6 dispatch illustrates. "Let your pickets chat enough not to tell them anything, but to find out his regiments."[32] Sgt. Orvey S. Barrett cites an example of idle chatter during picket duty. "The Johnnys were on one side of the river [Kelly's Ford], and we occupied the other, doing picket; a long, lankey Johnny sat on the bank of the stream, poorly dressed, with his feet in the water; no firing at this time, by mutual consent. One of our smart Alicks sung out to him. 'I say, Johnney Reb., why don't you wear better clothes?' His reply was prompt, 'We uns don't wear our best clothes when

---

29. *Ibid.*, June 4, 1863; Houghton journal, June 4, 1863.
30. *OR*, vol. 27, pt.3, p. 5, 9, 10-11.
31. Bancroft journal, June 6, 1863.
32. *OR*, vol. 27, pt. 3, p. 17.

Company H of the 4th Michigan

National Archives

The names of the individual soldiers are unknown. It is believed to be an early war photograph, as the soldier on the left end is wearing a fez cap and the soldier on the right end has the sword of a non-commissioned officer, yet he has no chevrons. This was not uncommon when a regiment was first formed. Of particular interest are the three vices of a soldier: smoking, playing cards and drinking, all three of which are clearly depicted here.

we go to kill hogs.'" The firing truce promptly ended. A very pleasant Saturday drew to a close with "rain in the pm."[33]

June 7 brought some relief from the daily routine for it was Sunday and a "divine service" took place at 4 p.m. Corporal Seage recalled that the chaplain, his father, had a "good sermon" which was entitled "Be troubled ye careless ones." One can almost hear the chaplain's admonitions to take heed of one's spiritual needs, particularly in time of war when one can not predict when a ball will strike him down: trust in the Lord, do not drink, do not gamble, try to live by His laws—do not jeopardize your Heavenly home. The soldiers on both sides of the conflict were largely a deeply devout group, so a sermon admonishing them not to be "careless" was quite appropriate.[34]

Monday, June 8 was an eventful day. Colonel Sweitzer received orders for the Second Brigade to report to Brig. Gen. David M. Gregg, who was commanding a division of cavalry and was under orders to lead a reconnaissance across the Rappahannock River and south to Mountain Run. Following the cavalry, the brigade became engaged. When the cavalry broke off the engagement the reconnaissance unit returned to the north bank of the Rappahannock. This same day changed the life forever of Chaplain John B. Seage. A forty-five-year-old Baptist minister born in England in 1809, had emigrated to America in 1839 and raised a family of five children. When the war erupted his eldest son, Richard Watson, enlisted in Company E as a corporal at the age of twenty-three and was mustered on June 20, 1861. Three months later on September 27 his brother Henry enlisted and joined Richard in Company E. The regiment was in need of a chaplain by July, 1862, so Chaplain Seage joined his two sons and was commissioned and mustered into the 4th Michigan on July 20, 1862, in Falmouth, Virginia.[35]

The Fifth Corps was assigned to guard the fords and roads around Kelly's Ford, including picket duty, patrols and reconnaissance. Their objective was primarily to guard against General Lee's Army of Northern Virginia but also to keep an ever watchful eye out for guerrillas or "bushwhackers." Bushwhackers posed a host of problems; they raided military installations

33. Orvey S. Barrett, *The Old 4th Michigan Infantry* (Detroit, Michigan: W. Ostler, 1888), p. 21. Barrett was twenty-six years old when he enlisted as sergeant of Company B on June 20, 1861. By February 28, 1863, he was commissioned second lieutenant, a rank he held until his disability discharge on account of wounds on May 23, 1864. *Record Fourth Michigan*, p. 10.
34. Seage journal, June 7, 1863; *ibid.*, June 8, 1863.
35. *OR*, vol. 27, p. 608; Brown, *Record Fourth Michigan*, p. 98.

and outposts and they captured or killed stragglers and mail carriers. The regiment had been without mail for almost three weeks so on that fateful day the chaplain volunteered to carry outgoing mail to Washington via Aquia Creek and to bring back mail. What Chaplain Seage carried, however, was more than mere letters, for he had with him $6,000 of the regiment's money to be sent back home to the boys' families.[36] Chaplain Seage described his adventure in a post-war letter to General Robertson:

Jonathan Robertson, Adjutant General
June 1, 1866

General,

I have the honor most respectfully to submit the following statement of the manner & occasions of my being wounded.

I left the regiment, 4th Michigan Volunteer Infantry, in which I was a chaplain on the morning of the 8th of June at 4 o'clock under orders from Major General Meade then in command of our corps [the Fifth], the regiment was on duty at Kelly's Ford, Virginia, to proceed to Washington D.C. to transmit moneys for the officers and men to their families in Michigan. I had in my haversack about 6,000 dollars beside several watches for repair. I was alone and on horseback when 12 miles from the camp near Deep Run Mill I was halted by a party of men who ordered me to halt and surrender. I asked by what authority? The leader replied in the name of Moseby's [sic] Cavalry. I replied "I don't recognize that authority and shant surrender." They [three bushwhackers] fired and one ball went through my right wrist breaking the ratius and cutting off the radial artery passed through my coat, vest and shirt causing a wound in the rib. Seeing if the gang was in front and rear I wheeled my horse or rather the horse turned when they fired again, one ball entering the point of the left shoulder breaking the clavical. It was cut out 13 inches from the place of entry. My horse jumped across a ditch and they fired a third time. One ball cut open my left ankle and another made a flesh wound in my thigh.

My horse being one best got away from them. I found both arms useless and the blood from the severed

36. Houghton journal, June 8, 1863. John Bancroft had given the chaplain $500 on June 7. Bancroft journal, June 8, 1863.

Steve Roberts Collection

Reverend John Seage

John Seage, a Methodist minister from White Pigeon, Michigan, entered the service of the 4th Michigan at Falmouth, Virginia, on July 10, 1862, for a three year term of service at the age of forty-five. He received his commission as chaplain on July 20, 1862. When the 4th Michigan was reorganized for its second enlistment period, Chaplain Seage was assigned to it effective July 26, 1864. He served as its chaplain until discharged at the end of his enlistment on May 26, 1866, in Detroit.

artery springing out a stream. Our Division train & commissary was about a mile back thither horse took me.

The guards of the trains belong to our regiment. They seeing me coming and having heard the firing ran to meet me. My sight had gone from the loss of blood but I heard one exclaim "My God tis our dear Chaplain." I was taken from my horse and through kind and skillful treatment I was in a condition to be moved when the army went to head off Lee on his way to Gettysburg. I was in an ambulance to Manassas & from there to Washington where my wounds were dressed. The wrist put up in splints & both arms in slings I was sent home by the surgeon Dr. Clymer for 60 days.

In the early spring during the failure of our army called "Burnsides Stick in the Mud" I caught cold on my lungs & brought on a settle asthma which I now have & from which I shall never be free until relieved by death. Before I went into the Army I was never sick. I am now in body 40 years older then I was 5 years ago. I am partially cripple in both arms & when the weather is wet or cold I almost die from difficulty to breathe.

                            I am your obt. sevt.
John Seage late chaplain 4th Mich. Vol. Infy.

P.S. I has forgotten to say I did not lose a cent or a cent worth of anything entrusted to me. J.S.[37]

Alexander D. Patrick of Detroit, who enlisted in Company B at the age of twenty-four on June 20, 1861, was a long time brigade mail carrier. His report adds another perspective to Chaplain Seage's encounter:

The postmaster of the 62d Pennsylvania was detailed to take my place [having requested an in-camp furlough]. He had two large bags of mail matter and some important letters for General Burnside, then commandant at Aquia Creek.[38] He was mounted on a fine gray horse, and was well armed, having two large Colt's revolvers and a carbine. I gave him his instructions and away he went, but he never got to the end of

---

37. John Seage to Jonathan Robinson, June 1, 1866, Michigan Historical Collection.
38. Patrick probably means General Hooker here.

his journey. He, horse, nor mail were ever heard from. A few days later after this circumstance Chaplain Seage, of my regiment, was going to Washington, and volunteered to take the mail to Aquia Creek. When the reverend old gentleman took the road, well mounted, we thought at least his sacred cloth would be safe from our rapacious foe; but he had only been gone a few hours when his horse came bounding back with our priest severely wounded, almost riddled with rebel irreligious bullets.[39]

Notes from Henry Seage and John Bancroft further identify the location of Chaplain Seage's ambush as being twelve miles from camp on the Fredericksburg Road and two and one half miles from Grove Church.[40]

On Tuesday, June 9 Lieutenant Bancroft rose at 2 a.m. to command a work party of fifty men assigned to Battery H of the 1st Artillery to provide "slashing for a battery and entrenching work all day." Corporal Seage gained permission to temporarily leave the regiment to search for and accompany his wounded father. Bancroft noted that troops and cavalry had crossed the river and engaged in a severe fight with the infantry on the left flank and cavalry on the right.[41]

Wednesday morning, June 10, Company K of the 4th Michigan received light marching orders with three days rations. The order was familiar; however, this time the men did form up and move out. Their objective was a smaller ford about three miles downriver from Kelly's Ford called, appropriately enough, Little Ford, now known as Field's Ford. The company was in search of bushwhackers and their trails across the river. The company had marched about two miles down a road running through a woods when they encountered "3 bushwhackers about 10 rods [55 feet] ahead of us at the forks of the road." Capt. James B. McLean gave the order to halt and "load at will." Private Houghton recalled they "didn't wait to count their motions either" but their prey escaped to fight another day.[42] One more mile brought them to their destination: Little Ford and a small open field. Captain McLean posted pickets at the river and in an old house that sat back from the ford. The

39. *Michigan in the War*, p. 232.
40. Houghton journal, June 8, 1863; Seage journal, June 8, 1863; Bancroft journal, June 8, 1863.
41. Seage journal, June 9, 1863; Bancroft journal, June 9, 1863. Henry Seage reported hearing "heavy cannonading" all day.
42. Houghton journal, June 10, 1863. A company commander could exercise control over the speed of loading weapons in addition to firing styles. The

reserve was allowed to lie on their guns between the two outposts. Houghton noted that since the objective was to catch bushwhackers, the men of Company K did not "have to walk any beat," rather, "we took bushwacker style for it." The day had grown progressively warmer but as night approached it became cool. For those companies that remained in camp, the day was much the same as the previous days, ending with a late afternoon inspection.[43]

Thursday, June 11 brought some relief from the warm weather of the preceding days yielding a cloudy and cool day. The men went about their morning duties with the sound of artillery rumbling in the distance to their right in the direction of Brandy Station. The men of the 4th also learned who was opposing them on the opposite banks of the Rappahannock River—the 4th North Carolina Cavalry. This news came from a deserter from Confederate picket duty.[44] Company K remained on picket duty at Little Ford. Private Houghton related a story of the tension experienced on picket duty:

> I had just got to snoozing [having returned to the reserve position between the old house and the river] my best when a sharp crack of a rifle was heard up to the old house. We jumped up, fell in and was up there

---

slowest and most disciplined method of controlling loading speed was exercised through a series of commands called "load in nine times." This was a series of nine commands: 1. Load—the rifle butt is placed on the ground between the feet with the hammer facing outward. The soldier places his right hand into his cartridge box. 2. Handle cartridge—the soldier places the powder end of the cartridge between his teeth. 3. Tear cartridge—the cartridge is torn and placed at the muzzle. 4. Charge cartridge—powder is poured down the barrel and the ball is pushed into the bore. The soldier then reaches for the rammer. 5. Draw rammer—the rammer is drawn, turned upside down, and placed on the ball in the bore. 6. Ram cartridge—The ball is rammed home. 7. Return rammer—the rammer is withdrawn from the barrel and returned to the rammer pipe. 8. Prime—the hammer is opened to the half cocked position and a percussion cap is placed on the cone. 9. Shoulder arms—the weapon is returned to the shoulder arms position in preparation for the ready-aim-fire series of commands. W. J. Hardee, *Hardee's Rifle and Light Infantry Tactics* (New York: Kane, 1862), pp. 32-36.

43. James B. McLean was twenty-eight years old when he enlisted as a sergeant in Company K on June 20, 1861, in Adrian. He received his commission to second lieutenant in the same company on January 29, 1862. Five months later he was commissioned as first lieutenant. McLean was promoted to captain of Company K on September 28, 1862, a rank he held until his disability discharge on April 21, 1864. Brown, *Record Fourth Michigan*, p. 73.
44. *OR*, vol. 27, pt. 3, p. 58.

in about two minutes. The soldier's name was Moses Baker that was on that post.[45] He said that he heard a noise in the brush a short distance from the house like someone walking. When he could see about where it was he fired at it. The noise soon stopped. We didn't care to go and look for his game but kept a sharp lookout for more. After this there was 3 men put on each picket post.[46]

The cold front passed through Kelly's Ford by Friday, June 12, and the warm weather returned. It proved to be a busy day for the soldiers of the Fifth Corps. Edward Taylor wrote that "there was a brilliant cavalry fight near here in which our boys clearly showed their superiority as cavalry to the cavalry of the enemy."[47] Meanwhile at Little Ford, three miles downriver from Kelly's Ford and the main regimental camp, Captain McLean led a reconnaissance patrol of six men further downriver to look for signs of Rebel movements:

> So we started out going on the east bank of the river going as close to the stream as possible to see if there had been any Rebs crossing in boats. When we got about two miles from the Little Ford we found a boat where some rebs had crossed, the boat and paddle was yet wet and from all appearance they had not been gone but a few minutes. Captain McLean picked up the paddle, knocked the back end of the boat and sent it a drift downstream and left the Johnnies to get back the best they could. One half mile further brought us to a large plantation. Here we was treated kindly and from all appearance they were Union people. We could buy any eatibles that we desired. Here we were met by a patrol from the US Ford, they reported everything to be all right downriver. Learning this we returned back to the Little Ford with our canteens filled with milk and our haversacks with cakes & pies that we had bought off the old planter. We also feasted on mulberrys and cherrys that grew along the bank of the Rappahannock.[48]

45. Moses Baker, who enlisted on June 20, 1861, at the age of twenty-one, served until his discharge on June 29, 1864, at the conclusion of his term of service. *Record Fourth Michigan*, p. 9.
46. Houghton journal, June 11, 1863.
47. Edward Taylor to Lottie Taylor, June 12, 1863, Michigan Historical Collection.
48. Houghton journal, June 12, 1863.

Such a culinary find; a soldier's dream come true, considering the normal faire of hardtack, coffee, and salt pork.

Back at Kelly's Ford, Edward Taylor wrote to his sister Lottie providing insight into regimental picket duty and the concept of a "mess." A mess represented a group of any number of soldiers that pooled their rations and foraging prizes for the good of the group. This was a common practice during the war. Edward Taylor related: "I told Annie that I had returned to the regiment and was Sergeant Major there of. I find it is not a very hard place and the prospect ahead is very fair. I tent with the Adjutant [Lt. Horatio G. Lumbard] who is a clever fellow. I mess with about sixteen officers and turn my rations in for payment."[49]

Saturday, June 13 was yet another warm day. Captain McLean's Company K returned from Little Ford to the main regimental camp at Kelly's Ford. The routine of camp life had an additional feature this day as Lieutenant Bancroft relates that clothing was issued. This was welcomed by the soldiers, for what better way to rid oneself of body lice, or greybacks, than by stripping off the old infected clothing, bathing and removing stubborn lice, donning new clothes and celebrating by burning the old wools. Word soon spread through the regiment "that the Rebs was moving Northwest going on the east side of the Blue Ridge Mountains distance some 10 or 12 miles west of Kelly's Ford." The rumor was soon verified by the engagement of cavalry and light artillery "sent there to learn if they intended a general movement." Private Houghton continued that the enemy was clearly on the move because "we plainly see all their movements by the smoke." Few could have been surprised when marching orders were received at 4 p.m. due to orders received by General Barnes from General Meade that read in part: "Concentrate your division, as before ordered, at Morrisville, with batteries and trains. Wait there till the cavalry relieve your pickets. Leave strong pickets at Ellis' and Kelly's. Await me at Grove Church, where I will be in a few hours." The men busied themselves with striking their tents, grabbing a bit of "hard bread" to eat and inspecting their arms.[50] By 7 p.m. the brigade was in column marching north towards Morrisville via Grove Church. After marching eight miles, the column halted at 11 p.m. and established camp for the night. It can be argued that veterans were surely accustomed to lengthy marches in the southern heat since they had survived the battles of the

---

49. Edward Taylor to Lottie, June 12, 1863, Michigan Historical Collection.
50. Houghton journal, June 13, 1863; Seage journal, June 13, 1863.

Peninsular Campaign and most recently Chancellorsville. Arguable, too, is the supposition that they could not have anticipated or predicted the length of the forthcoming forced march, the dwindling time they had to complete the march or the oppressive heat they would have to endure. For Saturday June 13 marked the beginning of the long road to Gettysburg—a distance exceeding 135 miles.[51]

On Sunday, June 14 the men of the 4th were up early and on the march again by 5 a.m., headed towards Catlett's Station on the Orange & Alexandria Railroad via Bristersburg arriving there by seven in the evening. The heat of the day was oppressive, reported a member of the 155th Pennsylvania: "the heat was so great and the sun so strong . . . that ambulances following the troops were frequently filled with sufferers from sunstroke and exhaustion from heat." The day ended with a hard thundershower, which at first must surely have been a relief from the heat and dust. The men's mettle for tolerating weather extremes was indeed thoroughly tested that day.[52]

Union troops found no relief from the heat of the 14th as they rose early on Monday, June 15 and began a twenty mile march at 5 a.m. to Bristoe Station and on to Manassas Junction. The Army of the Potomac received orders to maintain a position between Washington and the Army of Northern Virginia. Rumors soon spread through the ranks that a third Bull Run would soon be fought as Private Houghton noted: "it was thought by some that we were going to have a 3rd Bull Run fight." The rumor is given further credence by the deployment of the "artillery and infantry drawn up in a line facing toward the valley."[53]

The heat continued on Tuesday, June 16 as the regiment, remaining at Manassas and encamped along the Thoroughfare Gap Road, was assigned night picket duty on the left and west of Manassas down the railroad. Their password for the night was "Trenton"; "every man that came near our posts that night was halted and if he said Trenton we would let him pass, if not he was put in the care of the officer of the guard."[54]

Wednesday, June 17 was a scorching day. The heat wave continued unabated, creating an uncommonly warm season for early June. The *Hillsdale Standard*, a Michigan paper report-

---

51. *OR*, vol. 27, pt. 3, p. 92; *ibid.*, pt. 1, p. 141.
52. *Ibid.*, p. 103; *ibid.*, pt. 1, p. 141; John W. Schildt, *Roads To Gettysburg* (Parsons, West Virginia: McClain, 1978), p. 71.
53. *OR*, vol. 27, pt.1, p. 142; *ibid.*, pt. 3, p. 103; Seage journal, June 15, 1863.
54. Brown, *Record Fourth Michigan*, p. 3. Company I, the Trenton Volunteers, was raised in Trenton, Michigan.

ing on the conditions in Virginia, published a report on June 30, saying, "There has been but a very little rain this season, and everything has suffered for want of rain, springs are drying up, and so are the small streams, which causes a great scarcity of water, and through the section of country from which we have come there is not an over abundance of water at any time and an army like ours soon uses up what there is." The men in blue paid the price that day. The troops were aware that General Lee was marching north but how far north and what his objectives might be were speculative and a source of lively discussion. The *Hillsdale Standard* continued:

> It is thought throughout the Army that he [Lee] is getting himself into a trap of his own setting by going so far North, and that he had better remain on his own 'sacred soil' while Curtis militia [Pennsylvania state militia] give him battle in the front, Hooker will most likely bring up Lee's rear in double quick time. I think Hooker will make a good provost guard for General Lee.

Intelligence was received that Rebels were in force at Ashby Gap some forty to forty-five miles northwest of Manassas. Orders were issued; march at 3 a.m. via Centreville to Gum Springs, now called Arcola, a distance of twenty-five miles.[55] Heat, wool clothing, armaments, accoutrements, forced marching and the scarcity of water struck hard. The combined effect was further intensified as Private Houghton recorded that the "road was through a dense forest most of the way which made it very suffocating." Lieutenant Bancroft related that he had to "rest very often" and that "men fall out of the ranks every few moments." Twenty-two-year-old Sgt. William H. Jackson of Company I was one those who "fell out" but "caught up at night." Not all those who dropped out due to heat exhaustion were fortunate enough to regain their strength and rejoin their unit under their own strength. Private Houghton noted that it was a "frequent occurrence to see men by the side of the road fainting with sun stroke, the doctors done what they could for them but could not tend to them all." One of the unfortunate victims of the heat was the colonel of the 25th New York who "was so badly injured by sunstroke that he died before 8." The 32nd Massachusetts, part of the Second Brigade with the 4th Michigan, started the march with 230 men and ended the

---

55. *OR*, vol. 27, pt 1, p. 151; *ibid.*, p. 142.

march with 107, a further testimony to the effect of the heat on the endurance of the soldiers.[56]

This section of the march must surely have been a difficult passage for one soldier of the 4th in particular. On June 20, 1861, Joseph Burce was mustered into the service of the 4th Michigan in Adrian, Michigan, but Burce's hometown was Fairfax, Virginia. As the regiment passed through Centreville, Virginia, Burce must have been experiencing mixed feelings of loyalty to the army and a desire to see his home again, for Fairfax was a mere seven miles northeast of Centreville.[57]

The regiment finally arrived in camp some two miles west of Gum Springs on the road to Aldie at sundown.[58] Gum Springs was a very small town generally bereft of men, most of whom had left their homes behind to fight for the Confederate cause. Consequently, some reports of the time describe the buildings as being in need of repair and paint. The regiment undoubtedly left a trail of unwanted personal gear along the route such as blankets, coats, and knapsacks. They also left a trail of stragglers. Though it was not uncommon, straggling nonetheless was against Army regulations. Private Houghton wrote that "no one got punished" for straggling. The bigger problem with being a straggler was the ever present possibility of being taken prisoner by a Confederate soldier or by a Rebel dressed in civilian clothes. "At night they prowl around the country and should a stray soldier be seen he is pretty generally nabbed, and before he is aware of it, is a prisoner of war." Although "no one got punished," straggling was not looked upon favorably under normal circumstances by officers or soldiers. Consider the tasks that had to be performed by the soldiers who completed the march without falling out. Once the column stopped at Gum Springs the men present had to establish the camp site, gather wood for evening fires, cook rations, set picket duties and other such tasks that made a military camp secure. In short, a great deal of work would have been performed by those present, for which the stragglers benefitted without contributing their share of effort.[59]

Two weeks from this date, Thursday June 18, would find the 4th Michigan, 32nd Massachusetts and 62nd Pennsylvania in a desperate fight for their lives in the Wheatfield. They had no

56. Houghton journal, June 17, 1863; *Hillsdale Standard*, June 30, 1863; Bancroft journal, June 17, 1863; Parker, *Story of the Thirty-second Massachusetts*, p. 163.
57. Brown, *Record Fourth Michigan*, p. 20.
58. *OR*, vol. 27, pt. 3, p. 174.
59. Schildt, *Roads to Gettysburg*, pp. 139-40; Houghton journal, June 17, 1863.

idea when they would engage Lee's army or where, but based solely on the recent series of forced marches and cavalry encounters, they surely knew that a major battle would erupt soon. The Fifth Corps left Gum Springs and advanced along the Winchester Turnpike within two miles of Aldie, halted and set up camp near sundown. From this base they provided support to Maj. Gen. Alfred Pleasonton's cavalry who was guarding the army's flank.[60] The Third Corps remained in Gum Springs with the Eleventh and Twelfth Corps between the Third and Fifth along the road to Leesburg. Maj. John S. Mosby's guerrilla force apparently was causing problems for the Union army. This is evident in Maj. Gen. Daniel Butterfield's June 18 dispatch to General Meade which read in part, "Catch and kill any guerrillas, then try them, will be a good method of treating them."[61] The heat continued that day and the evening became very still.

Friday, June 19, the heat finally broke and in its place came rain and a great deal of mud. Lieutenant Bancroft described the weather as "very disagreeable." The regiment received light marching orders so knapsacks were piled and guards detailed to watch them. The regiment was "in company with some cavalry and light artillery in pursuit of the Rebels driving them back seven miles west of Aldie [near Middleburg]. Here we halted, waited 2 or 3 hours . . . and returned to Aldie."[62] The engagement mentioned is a cavalry fight near Ashby Gap approximately ten miles west of Middleburg. The soldiers, ever mindful of opportunities to forage or buy good food, passed by a small mill on their return to Aldie from Middleburg. A mill meant flour and flour meant bread and gravy. Thoughts quickly turned towards visions of a good dinner. Private Houghton related what took place at dusk:

> The boys thought that it would be a good chance to get some flour to make gravy. So they made a rush for the mill pushing and crowding like a flock of sheep to see who would get their flour first. Some of the greedy ones that was a little behind the rest would put ten cents in their cup and reach it by the rest to get it filled with the precious stuff. There was three men in there dealing it out to the boys as fast as they could. As fast as their cups were filled they would start on a run to catch up with their companies. They did not go far till

60. *OR*, vol 27, pt.3, p. 191.
61. *Ibid.*, p. 194.
62. Bancroft journal, June 19, 1863.

they discovered that their cups felt heavy. A little closer examination convinced them that it was plaster of paris that they had been buying. A few cuss words were uttered over the matter.... This was too big a joke for our boys to receive without a little retaliation. As good luck had it we did not go but 80 rods from the mill till our regiment went into camp for the night. Here we found plenty of rails to build our fires with. We cooked and ate our suppers without any flour gravy. During the evening there was quite a discussion among the boys in regard to how they would get even with the men at the mill. Some thought it would serve them right to burn the mill. After the people in the town [by the mill] had gone to bed and everything was quiet some of the boys went back to the mill. Nearby sat quite a number of good fat hives of bees.[63] The best one was selected, tied up in a blanket and brought into our camp. Now came the tug of war. They were Rebel bees and of course they were fighting fellows. When the blanket was untied they came out by battalions, forming, charging on our company in a close hand to hand encounter which caused a smarting sensation nearly equal to Rebel sharpshooters. Our little company was greatly outnumbered and had to retreat and take up a new position on the opposite side of the fire. After awhile there was a smudge made and the bees were subdued. The honey was divided among the boys that bought plaster paris for flour. The boys seemed to feel that they had got their money back and left the mill unmolested.[64]

By three o'clock in the afternoon the 4th received marching orders, proceeded through Aldie, a distance of four miles, and established a new camp.[65]

Saturday, June 20, was a birthday of sorts since the regiment had been mustered into service on June 20, 1861. Two of the three year's enlistment period had been completed. The rain continued but that did not stop a few enterprising fellows from foraging. Private Houghton wrote:

> After roll call was over a fellow in Company G and myself went downtown to see if we could buy some

63. Honey was a luxury to the soldiers and hives were a valuable asset to the hives' owner.
64. Houghton journal, June 19, 1863.
65. *OR*, vol. 27, pt.1, p. 53.

eatables. We hunted the little town over but could find nothing. On our return back we discovered a nice herd of cows in a wheatfield. We thought perhaps some of them was suffering for want of being milked so we examined the cows and found it just as we expected. The one that had the largest bag was selected and drove up in the corner of the fence. I stood guard over the cow while my comrade done the milking. We drank what we could, filled our canteens and started for camp. We had not gone far till we found where some heartless fellow had killed a calf. As we did not want the meat to lay there and spoil we skinned the hind legs and each one of us took a ham and started for camp with the expectation of dividing our veal among the boys. But to our surprise when we got back the regiment had gone, not a blue coat was in sight. We was then well aware of the danger we was in being gobbled up or shot by bushwhackers. We cut off a few slices of veal threw them on the coals and while they were roasting we cut what meat we could from our hams put it in our haversacks and started in pursuit of our regiment.[66]

The regiment had returned to the camp of the 19th during the period these two soldiers were foraging.

On Sunday, June 21, the steady rain of the previous day subsided and was replaced by occasional showers. The First Division was up early having received marching orders at 3 a.m. It proceeded through Aldie Gap towards Middleburg and Upperville.[67] The area had been touched little by the ravages of war; consequently, the foraging was very good on this march. Lieutenant Bancroft recorded that there were "plenty of pigs and chickens" and cherries. The division stopped briefly in Middleburg after a march of six miles to await further orders. General Barnes received orders to report to General Pleasonton in support of his cavalry for an excursion to Ashby Gap, where the Rebels were reportedly moving in a northern direction. General Barnes ordered the Third Brigade under Col. Strong Vincent and the 3rd Massachusetts Battery C to proceed with the cavalry and for the First and Second Brigades to march "to the woods" beyond Middleburg and remain in camp. It is interesting to note that orders issued on June 20 had requested "that you detach two brigades of infantry from your corp to support

66. Houghton journal, June 20, 1863.
67. Seage journal, June 21, 1863; *OR*, vol. 27, pt. 3, p. 229; *ibid.*, pt.1, p. 142.

this movement."⁶⁸ Barnes detached one brigade of infantry and one battery. Later in the day one soldier made note of the "heavy cannonading off in the valley" as Pleasonton's cavalry, under General Gregg with the accompaniment of the Third Brigade, engaged Maj. Gen. J.E.B. Stuart's cavalry in Ashby Gap. Private Houghton relates another example of foraging. In this one, however, note the difference in respect for property owned by officers of the Confederate army:

> One day as we were going through the northern part of Virginia we halted for a short time in the door yard of an old planter. The boys learned by some of the negroes that the old planter was an officer in the Rebel Army, so the boys did not care what they done. In the yard close by the house were some very nice cherry trees filled with cherries. One of the boys said it was not necessary for the whole company to climb after cherries so he took his hatchet, climbed to the top of the tree and began trimming. The heavy load were soon all dropped to the ground where our company could have free access to them. Other trees where served the same way till the boys got all they wanted. We then started on without asking the occupants of the house how they liked the trimming.⁶⁹

The day ended with a light shower and the boys enjoying mutton, milk and cherries along with their coffee. Company H was detailed to picket duty during the night.⁷⁰

At army headquarters, General Butterfield received positive identification of the location of the Army of Northern Virginia and their movement as reported by Maj. Gen. Henry Slocum of the Twelfth Corps near Leesburg. "A deserter from [Maj. Gen. George E.] Pickett's division, [Lt. Gen. James] Longstreet's corp, came in this evening. Longstreet's corps is near Snicker's Gap. [Maj. Gen. Lafayette] McLaws' division is at Ashby's Gap. He says the rebel soldiers think [Lt. Gen. Richard S.] Ewell's corps is in Maryland, and that [Lt. Gen. A. P.] Hill's corps is in rear of Longstreet's, but is to follow on; that the whole army is to go into Maryland."⁷¹

The rain of the previous days had moved on, leaving in its wake mud that would dry as the warm weather returned to

---

68. *Ibid.*, p. 598; *ibid*, pt. 3, p. 248; *ibid.*, p. 229.
69. Houghton journal, June 21, 1863.
70. Bancroft journal, June 21, 1863.
71. *OR*, vol. 27, pt.3, p. 249.

northern Virginia. It was Monday, June 22 and the 4th Michigan remained in camp beyond Middleburg while the Third Brigade under Colonel Vincent continued in support of General Pleasonton's cavalry at Ashby Gap. By late afternoon Sweitzer's brigade moved up to relieve Vincent's brigade as the First Division began falling back to its camp at Aldie. Sweitzer's Second Brigade and the 3rd Massachusetts Battery C, acting as rear guard, were kept busy skirmishing with the Rebels who followed but not in force. The First and Third Brigades returned to Aldie followed by the Second Brigade which arrived in the evening. Lieutenant Bancroft noted that the regiment "lay all night in line of battle" as a rumor spread that General Longstreet had reinforced his troops west of Middleburg.[72]

By the morning of Tuesday, June 23, the entire First Division was reunited with the balance of the Fifth Corps, encamped at Aldie. Recall that the Third Corps was at Gum Springs and the Eleventh and Twelfth Corps were on the right of the Fifth along the road to Leesburg. Rumors continued to abound with reports of General Lee at Leesburg to the north and Rebel pickets to the southeast at Manassas. A third rumor, or perhaps a wish, was recorded by Lieutenant Bancroft: "Probably Lee is sending men west [to Vicksburg] under cover of this raid." From this same letter insight is gained into how the Middleburg area appeared; "fine farming country ... nice stone walls to fight over ... good hills for artillery."[73] By this time the story of the Fifth Corps' near success of ambushing and capturing Mosby on June 22 may have been circulating through the corps. General Meade reported the attempt to Maj. Gen. Oliver O. Howard:

> I came near catching our friend Mosby this morning. I had reliable intelligence of his expected passing a place about 4 miles from here at sunrise. I sent 40 mounted men (all I have) and 100 infantry, who succeeded in posting themselves in ambush at the designated spot. Sure enough, Mr. Mosby, together with 30 of his followers, made their appearance about sunrise, but, I regret to say, their exit also, from what I can learn, through the fault both of foot and horse. It appears Mosby saw the cavalry, and immediately charged them. They ran (that is, my horses) toward the infantry, posted behind

---

72. *Ibid.*, pt.1, p. 599; John Bancroft to Mr. Hinchman, June 23, 1863, Burton Collection.
73. *Ibid.*

a fence. The infantry, instead of rising and deliberately delivering their fire, fired lying on the ground; did not hit a rebel, who immediately scattered and dispersed, and thus the prettiest chance in the world to dispose of Mr. Mosby was lost.[74]

The day ended with the regiment on picket duty.

The boys of Company H were on picket duty on Wednesday, June 24, except for Lieutenant Bancroft, who reported to sick call with diarrhea. Bancroft went on to record that "we are in good spirit and discipline but would like to get into some shop to get a change of clothes and something to live on beside hardtac, coffee, fresh beef." The big event for the day was the return of Corporal Seage who had accompanied his wounded father to Washington. Seage had started from Centreville at 7 a.m. and arrived at Aldie at 2 p.m. while Company I was on picket duty. He noted that he had a cold nights' sleep as he only had a rubber blanket and a piece of poncho for covering, both of which are rubber coated and good for protection against wet weather but poor heat insulators.[75]

Thursday, June 25 dawned cloudy and a cool fifty-nine degrees at 7 a.m., according to Gettysburg College's Reverend Dr. Michael Jacobs' weather log. Camp life continued which including the washing of clothes as Henry Seage recorded. Lt. Col. George Lumbard requisitioned armaments and supplies from the quartermaster for Company H including eleven cartridge boxes, fourteen cap boxes, fifteen waist belts, fifteen U.S. belt plates, fifteen bayonet scabbards, three eagle breast plates and 2,287 rounds of .58 caliber ammunition. These supplies he turned over to William Robinson for distribution. At sixty rounds per person, the 2,287 rounds were enough for about thirty-eight men.[76]

By the evening of the 25th, the temperature was sixty-three degrees and the heavens opened up with a heavy rainstorm, making cooking fires nearly impossible to kindle.[77]

---

74. *OR*, vol. 27, pt. 3, p. 255.
75. Bancroft journal, June 24, 1863; Seage journal, June 24, 1863.
76. Michael Jacobs, "Meteorology of the Battle," *Gettysburg Magazine*, no. 10 (July 1994): 120-21; Seage journal, June 25, 1863. George W. Lumbard was commissioned captain of Company E on May 16, 1861, at the age of thirty-one. By July 1, 1862, he was promoted to the rank of lieutenant colonel which he held until his appointment to colonel on July 3, 1863. George W. Lumbard died of wounds received at the Wilderness on May 5, 1864. Brown, *Record Fourth Michigan*, p. 71.
77. Schildt, *Roads to Gettysburg*, p. 205; Seage journal, June 25, 1863.

Chapter Three
Double Quicking to Gettysburg

On Friday, June 26, the march to Gettysburg began in earnest. During the next six days the Fifth Corps covered over 100 miles, or an average of 16 miles per day. The soldiers wore wool pants, muslin shirts, wool socks, heavy shoes called brogans, wool vests, and four-button wool sack coats or nine-button frock coats. In addition, they wore waistbelts with U.S. brass belt buckles, cartridge box slings with brass eagle breastplates, cartridge boxes with up to sixty rounds of ammunition, cap pouches with at least seventy-two caps, bayonets and scabbards, canteens and haversacks that contained all sorts of personal items, including rations. On their backs or slung over their shoulder would be a blanket, a gum blanket or poncho and one half of a shelter tent.[1] Finally, the soldier also carried his weapon, generally a Springfield rifle weighing approximately ten pounds. The total weight of this combination of clothing and gear would have been staggering, and this is important to keep in mind. In the ensuing days the weight of all this gear, in concert with the heat and forced marches, would take its toll.

The Fifth Corps was up and prepared to march north by 4 a.m. on Friday, June 26, 1863. By 7 a.m. the 4th Michigan was on the road toward Leesburg, Virginia. The temperature was cool, making the march tolerable.[2] At Carter Mill on Goose Creek, south of Leesburg, the regiment stopped for a one hour rest. The time was used to relax, boil coffee and eat whatever they carried in their haversacks. The Fifth Corps continued the march north through Leesburg to Edwards Ferry, located on

---

1. A shelter tent, also called a dog tent, was a two-man, open-ended tent. Each soldier carried one half of a tent. The two sections were buttoned along one seam and erected using a ridge pole and two Y-shaped end poles about three and one half feet tall or men could simply roll up in their half.
2. Seage journal, June 26, 1863; *OR*, vol. 27, pt. 3, p. 314; Jacobs, "Meteorology of the Battle," pp. 120-21. The temperature in Leesburg was probably ten degrees more or less than the sixty-three degrees recorded in Gettysburg at 2 p.m.

the Potomac approximately thirty miles from Washington. At this point, the Potomac was 1,500 feet wide and was crossed via a pontoon bridge that the army erected. The 4th Michigan marched an additional seven miles after crossing the Potomac to within four miles of the mouth of the Monocacy River. There the regiment halted for the night at 9 p.m.; the men had been awake for seventeen hours and had marched for fourteen. It had been a long and hard thirty mile march. Lieutenant Bancroft recorded that there was some rain on "one of the most tiresome marches of the war." Henry Seage also recorded that he "was very tired" after the march. One good thing Henry Seage of Company I did during the march, however, was to stop in Leesburg long enough to "buy $7.00 worth of tobacco for the company." The dangers of straggling continued to exist as pension records attest for twenty-three-year-old Luke Barnes of Company C, who fell out of ranks due to being "sunstruck and unfit for duty." The brigade surgeon ordered him to be made comfortable and left behind. He was captured, imprisoned at Libby Prison and subsequently paroled and returned to the regiment on January 1, 1864. Luke Barnes served out his three year enlistment until being mustered out on June 30, 1864, in Detroit.[3]

Saturday, June 27 found the regiment in marching formation by 6 a.m. It arrived two miles from the mouth of the Monocacy River by noon, then moved upriver to find a suitable crossing, where it crossed the river and stopped for dinner.[4] It proved to be a long, welcomed rest for the regiment as the march was not resumed until five in the afternoon. The line of march took the men through Buckeystown within two miles of the southern edge of Frederick, Maryland, where the regiment made camp along Billenger's Creek. The day's march was not as long as the previous day's; however, the men were tired and straggling continued. The combined effect of long marches, heat, and the weight of their gear was beginning to show. Thirty-year-old Sgt. John Dean of Company H fell out of line, rested and eventually secured a ride in a wagon. Sometime after leaving the wagon he realized he left his gear in it. He was charged $22.50 for the lost equipment. Twenty-three-year-old Pvt. Riley E. Vanzile and Pvt. Jackson Smith of Company K

---

3. *OR*, vol. 27, pt.1, p. 143; Schildt, *Roads to Gettysburg*, p. 245; Bancroft journal, June 26, 1863; Seage journal, June 26, 1863; Luke Barnes, Pension Records, National Archives; Brown, *Record Fourth Michigan*, p. 10.
4. Bancroft journal, June 27, 1863; Seage journal, June 27, 1863.

Steve Roberts Collection

Henry Seage

Henry Seage, second son of Chaplain John Seage, enlisted in Company E in Hudson on September 27, 1861, for three years at the age of seventeen. Henry Seage held the ranks of corporal and color sergeant, receiving the latter on November 2, 1863. He was discharged on September 10, 1864, at the expiration of his term of service.

were reported missing and never returned to the regiment. Twenty-one-year-old Pvt. Henry Train of Company K was a new recruit who joined the regiment at Falmouth in March as a substitute for John W. Moon who was drafted on February 10, 1863. Private Train deserted on this leg of the march. The day ended with General Order Number 194 being issued which read in part "By direction of the President, Major General Joseph Hooker is relieved of command of the Army of the Potomac, and Major General George G. Meade is appointed to the command of that Army and of the troops temporarily assigned to duty with it." It was signed "By order of the Secretary of War. E.D. Townsend Adjutant General."[5]

At 2 a.m. on Sunday, General Meade received orders that he had been placed in command of the Army of the Potomac. Maj. Gen. George Sykes assumed command of the Fifth Corps. General Meade accepted the position with some trepidation, recognizing that President Lincoln was continuing his search for a commanding general who could bring victory to the North and draw the war to a successful completion. His predecessor's success and longevity was well known to him.

The Fifth Corps remained still on Sunday, June 28 regaining its strength and allowing the change in command to be implemented. It was a rainy day with the temperature rising to sixty-seven degrees by 2 p.m. The regiment was off duty. Cpl. Henry Seage seized the opportunity and went to Frederick and bought "lots of tobacco." Frederick was easily found due to the clearly visible landmarks of five church spires rising higher than any of the surrounding buildings. He returned in the afternoon in time for mail call when he received a package containing one letter and a pair of shoes. It was the first mail received by the regiment in many days. By 10 p.m. the Second Brigade was placed on picket duty.[6]

The Second Brigade returned to camp at 6 a.m. and resumed the march north at 8 a.m. on Monday, June 29. Henry Seage recorded that the army took two routes; one through and one around Frederick. The army reformed east of the city, crossed the Monocacy River and continued on through Mt. Pleasant where it halted for dinner. After a dinner break, the army continued the march until it established its camps at 7 p.m. two

5. *OR*, vol. 27, pt 1, p. 143; Brown, *Record Fourth Michigan*, pp. 101, 111, 114.
6. Captain Robinson's report, August 31, 1863, Michigan Historical Collection; *OR*, vol. 27, pt. 3, p. 369; *ibid.*, pt. 1, p. 375; Schildt, *Roads to Gettysburg*, p. 247; Jacobs, "Meteorology of the Battle," pp. 120-21; Seage journal, June 28, 1863.

miles east of Liberty, Maryland, towards Johnsville after having marched fifteen miles. Tension was building and tempers rose as Lieutenant Seage recorded a fight between two soldiers in Company E. "Frank [Francis] Waller and George Walker had a little row. [Second Lt. George L.] Maltz parted them by knocking Frank down with his sword, then Frank knocked Walker down cutting a large gash under his eye." The day ended with a hard rain and a cool sixty-nine degrees at 9 p.m.[7]

Tuesday, June 30 began very early with the troops rising at 4 a.m. General Sykes marched his men twenty-eight miles in accordance to General Meade's orders. The regiment left the Liberty camp early "without breakfast" and marched toward Union Mills, where Rebel cavalry had been reported. Tension and expectations began to rise again as a circular from the headquarters of the Army of the Potomac was distributed that directed "corp commanders will hold their commands in readiness at a moment's notice . . . the men must be provided with three days ration in haversacks and with sixty rounds of ammunition in the boxes and upon the person."[8]

The route of advance took the Army through Unionville, Johnsville, Union Bridge, Uniontown, Frizzellburg and Union Mills. As Company F passed through Uniontown twenty-one-year-old William Hamp, the brigade commissary, fell out of line. Company F continued the march, assuming that Hamp was a straggler who would catch up when the 4th established camp for the night. Hamp never caught up however, and he was never heard from again. Henry Seage recorded that skirmishers were kept two miles out during the march and established camp at 4 p.m. in the afternoon along Pipe Creek. It had been a warm day for such a long march with the temperature climbing to seventy-nine degrees by 2 p.m.[9] Henry Seage recorded that his supper consisted of "raddish and onions" and John Bancroft noted that he had an opportunity to "wash in a rapid stream." Along the way they learned that J.E.B. Stuart's cavalry had passed through Union Mills at 10 a.m. The expectation

7. *Ibid.*; *OR*, vol. 27, pt. 3, p. 375; *ibid.*, pt. 1, p. 144; Seage journal, June 29, 1863.
8. *OR*, vol. 27, pt. 3, p. 417. Sixty rounds of ammunition were six arsenal packs. Each arsenal pack contained ten rounds and twelve percussion caps. The rounds were wrapped in paper and generally tied with a string. When the arsenal packs were opened and the rounds put into the cartridge box, the wrapping paper would be retained by many of the soldiers for a variety of purposes including writing letters.
9. *OR*, vol. 27, pt.1, p. 144; *ibid.*, pt. 3, pp. 424, 402; Brown, *Record Fourth Michigan*, p. 53; Seage journal, June 30, 1863; Jacobs, "Meteorology of the Battle," pp. 120-21.

of battle must surely have loomed; when and where, however, was still a matter of speculation.

Private Houghton noted that "the nearer the [Pennsylvania] state line we got the more for the Union they appeared to be." He went on to cite an example of civilian enthusiasm they experienced while passing through Unionville: "As we passed through the last named town [Unionville] we kept step by the beat of the drums. The ladies and children were on the porches waving the Stars and Stripes and singing the Star Spangled Banner. Also a number of other patriotic songs equally as good. This made us forget our tired limbs and sore feet for awhile. We were not usually greeted in this kind of way when in Rebel country." A similar example is related in *The History Of The Fifth Army Corps:* "One good woman, we wish we had remembered her name, on the road from Frederick to Union Mills, stood at her table all day long making the celebrated Maryland biscuits, and as fast as a panful was baked sent them by her children to the gateway, where two or three were given to each soldier as he passed."[10] Surely such positive public demonstrations were an inspiration to the men of the 4th as they continued their march to Gettysburg and their date with destiny.

---

10. Houghton journal, June 30, 1863; William Henry Powell, *History of the Fifth Army Corps* (New York: Putnam, 1896; reprint, Dayton, Ohio: Morningside, 1984), p. 509.

Chapter Four
The Battle of Gettysburg

The morning of the battle call, to every soldier
  dear!
Oh joy, the cry is forward! Oh joy, the foe is
  near!
For all the crafty men of peace have failed to
  purge the land;
Hurrah! the ranks of battle close! God takes his
  cause in hand.[1]

Before Wednesday, July 1 was over the Fifth Corps would be encamped on the outskirts of Gettysburg. Camp was broken by 6 a.m. and the First Division, after drawing rations, left Union Mills by 9 a.m. bound for Hanover, Pennsylvania, a distance of fourteen miles.[2] As the regiment crossed the Mason-Dixon Line into Pennsylvania, Colonel Jeffords brought it to a halt:

> The order was then given to stack arms.[3] Colonel Jeffords said "Men you are now standing on free soil once more. Now give three cheers for the free soil states." This was done and if I ever heard the woods ring with cheers it was then. It was then imagined that we breathed purer air. In short time the command "attention take arms" was given and we were soon filing out in the direction of Gettysburg. The Rebels

---

1. Robertson, *Michigan in the War*, p. 420.
2. Seage journal, July 1, 1863; *OR*, vol. 27, pt.1, p. 144.
3. "Stack arms" refers to the process by which a pyramid of three muskets is created by interlocking them at the point of the curve in the bayonet just above the muzzle. Additional muskets could then by leaned on the original three. This was the standard method for storing muskets while the soldiers were still in formation. The process assured a neat, orderly camp and the return of the soldiers to their proper place in line when the command "fall in" was heard.

Monroe County Historical Commission

Harrison H. Jeffords

Harrison H. Jeffords, of Dexter was a twenty-four-year-old lawyer when President Lincoln's call for volunteers was heard. He enlisted in Company K of the 4th Michigan, receiving his commission as first lieutenant on May 16, 1861, and was mustered into service in Adrian on June 20, 1861. He was the 4th's second colonel, succeeding Colonel Woodbury.

were now roaming at will over the free soil of Pennsylvania and they were going to give us a battle on free soil and see how we would like it. We were all well aware that a hard battle was soon to be fought.[4]

James Houghton's observations of an upcoming "hard battle" were further reinforced as he and all of the Fifth Corps viewed the bodies of men and horses and homes damaged by artillery fire from the cavalry battle of the previous day that took place along the very road they were traveling. The route, however, did take them through territory that was unaffected by the cavalry battle of June 30; as Lieutenant Bancroft observed, there were "splendid farms and large barns."[5]

The Fifth Corps marched in seventy-six degree heat arriving in the vicinity of Hanover, between three and four in the afternoon and "stacked arms briefly." Some time during the course of the day's march, twenty-year-old Alanson R. Piper of Company B received word that he had been promoted to corporal. Within twenty-four hours his newly appointed leadership responsibilities would be soundly tested. Cpl. Henry Seage noted that the 4th Michigan "turned in to the fields one mile from Hanover" and set up camp. The pace of the march from Union Mills had been very rapid. As a member of the 155th Pennsylvania recalled, "Only the hardiest could endure the gait, and many fell out exhausted." The men thought their day's march was over, even though the "roar of battle" sounding in the distance could be heard as they approached Hanover, thus tents where set up and fires started so that they could have a good evening meal. Even commissary officers assumed the day had ended, for cattle were slaughtered for distribution to the men.[6]

Their hopes for a long rest were dashed when General Meade issued orders to General Sykes at 7 p.m.: "The Major-General commanding directs that you move up to Gettysburg at once upon receipt of this order, if not already ordered to do so by General Slocum." By 7 p.m. the tents had been struck and the Fifth Corps was on the march again heading toward Gettysburg, a distance of "some 12 or 13 miles."[7]

4. Houghton journal, July 1, 1863.
5. Bancroft journal, July 1, 1863.
6. Jacobs, "Meteorology of the Battle," pp. 120-21; Brown, *Record Fourth Michigan*, p. 88; Henry Seage journal, July 1, 1863; Schildt, *Roads to Gettysburg*, p. 71; Jim Houghton journal, July 1, 1863. On July 1, 1865, as a member of Company D of the Reorganized 4th, Piper was made sergeant.
7. *OR*, vol. 27, pt. 3, p. 467; *ibid.*, p. 483.

A rumor spread through the ranks that Gen. George B. McClellan had once again been put in command.⁸ This seemed to have a positive effect on the men for General McClellan continued to be held in high regard by the soldiers. However, it was only a rumor, started perhaps to bolster morale, for as an army commander, General Meade was untested. Within the ranks of the Fifth Corps, Meade was known as a fighter. That reputation, however, may not have been known throughout the other corps. Consequently, it could be argued that he was untested in their eyes. The McClellan rumor took on even more significance for bolstering morale. By midnight the 4th Michigan had marched an additional nine miles. Private Barrett wrote that it was a "beautiful moonlight night" and that "people came out with water and refreshments."⁹ Lieutenant Bancroft recorded hearing "heavy firing westward" and of being "very tired" at the end of the day's march, which had begun fifteen hours earlier. Twenty-four-year-old Pvt. Moses A. Luce, from McDonough, Illinois, of Company E wrote that "[we] slept on our arms in the vicinity of the battlefield during the night."¹⁰ James Houghton wrote, "We were too tired to cook any supper so we ate a cold lunch which consisted of raw pork, hard tack and sun cooked coffee. We then laid down to what rest we could. . . . We were well aware that the next day would be a day of bloodshed and that with some of us our next sleep would be the cold sleep of death. During the night we were frequently awakened by the arrival of other troops coming in and taking their positions. The heavy tread of infantry, the rattling of canteens and the command of officers was heard all night." The men of the 4th Michigan, weary from a forced twenty mile march from Union Mills, Maryland, pulled off to the side of the road, in the woods three to four miles east of Gettysburg, lay on their arms and fell asleep.¹¹

By 4 a.m. on July 2, 1863, the men were up, undergoing arms inspection and on the march again by daylight, eating whatever they could along the way for they started "without eating breakfast," with the Second Brigade leading the way for the First Division, marching via McSherrytown.¹² By 7 a.m. they

8. Barrett, *Old Fourth Michigan* , p. 21.
9. *OR*, vol. 27, pt.1, p. 610; *ibid.*, pt. 3, p. 483; Barrett, *Old Fourth Michigan*, p. 21.
10. Bancroft journal, July 1, 1863; Moses A. Luce journal, July 1, 1863, Edgar A. Luce Collection, San Diego, California.
11. Houghton journal, July 1, 1863; *OR*, vol. 27, pt.1, p. 610.
12. Seage journal, July 2, 1863; Houghton journal, July 2, 1863; *OR*, vol. 27, pt. 3, p. 483; *ibid.*, pt.1, pp. 144, 610.

had arrived "near the right of the line near a farmhouse and barn . . . in the immediate neighborhood of General Meade." There, "the Fifth Corps, pending the arrival of the Sixth [Corps] was held in reserve." The farm used was the Deardorff farm on Brinkerhoff Ridge about two miles east of Gettysburg along the Hanover Road. The First Division was massed and deployed left to right as follows: Third Brigade - Second Brigade - First Brigade "in a field not far from Wolf's Hill." The 9th Massachusetts, Second Brigade, was detached for picket duty.[13] The 9th may have been chosen for picket duty due to their type of muskets. They were armed with .69 caliber smoothbore muskets. Capt. William F. Robinson of Company F utilized his time to requisition supplies including "seven Springfield rifled muskets, seven bayonet scabbards, seven caps boxes & cone picks, seven cartridge boxes, seven waist belts, seven waist belt plates, 320 rounds elongated ball cartridges."[14]

The Fifth Corps remained in the rear and east of the right end of the Union line pending orders to support the Twelfth Corps. The First Division marched south along present day Highland Avenue, winding along the east side of Wolf's Hill until it intersected the Baltimore Pike. They arrived in their new position, "in the orchard just above the stone bridge on the Baltimore Pike," by 1 p.m. and "lay quietly til about 3 o'clock in the afternoon, when we went to the front" according to a letter written by Lt. John Bancroft. While in this position General Sykes received orders to move to the left, to support Maj. Gen. Daniel E. Sickles' Third Corps, which was thought to be holding the left along a line running from the end of Cemetery Ridge to Big Round Top. General Sickles was assumed to be occupying the pivotal defensive position of Little Round Top.[15] The day had grown progressively warmer and uncomfortable for the men were exposed to the "hot sun." The Reverend Dr. Michael

---

13. *Ibid.*, pp. 116, 610.
14. Arms Requisition Form No. 7, Michigan Historical Collection. William F. Robinson, from Hillsdale County, was twenty-four years old when he was mustered into service in Company H on June 20, 1861, as first sergeant. On December 12, 1861, he received a promotion to second lieutenant then to first lieutenant by July 18, 1862. He was in command of Company F from October 30, 1862, subsequently receiving a promotion to captain on January 27, 1863. His term of service ended on May 21, 1864, just thirty days before his scheduled expiration, via disability discharge on account of wounds received in action. Brown, *Record Fourth Michigan*, p. 94.
15. *OR*, vol. 27, pt.1, p. 592; John Bancroft to Michigan Adjutant General, June 17, 1889, Heckert Collection, Monroe Historical Museum, Monroe, Michigan.

Jacobs of the Pennsylvania College in Gettysburg had recorded a temperature of eighty-one degrees at 2 p.m.[16]

The front referred to by Lieutenant Bancroft was not the line running from Cemetery Ridge to the Round Tops. General Sickles, on his own authority, had vacated his assigned position and advanced to a lower ridge anchored on the left by an outcropping of huge boulders, now referred to as Devil's Den, extending to the right through Rose's Woods and anchored against the stone fence separating the woods from a wheatfield. Brig. Gen. J. H. Hobart Ward's brigade was placed in this position. A second line of defense ran approximately east and west along Stony Hill due west of the Wheatfield. This position was assigned to Col. Regis de Trobriand's Third Brigade of Maj. Gen. David B. Birney's First Division. The colonel deployed his men on the slope of Stony Hill with the 17th Maine anchoring his left behind a stone fence facing south. Behind Colonel de Trobriand and at a right angle facing west was the 40th New York. To the right of Colonel de Trobriand was Brig. Gen. Charles K. Graham's brigade in the Peach Orchard; a distance of some 300 yards.[17]

General Meade learned of the weakness in the Union left and ordered General Sykes to the left and to "hold it at all hazard." Within an hour of this order, the men of the 4th would find themselves in the most desperate and devastating fight for their very lives they had yet seen. James Houghton wrote, "We was ordered to fall in and was then furnished with 20 extra rounds of cartridges which we put in our haversacks where we could get them handy." The men were now carrying up to eighty rounds, enough for forty minutes or more of sustained firepower. Keep in mind that the speed of loading and firing decreased as the number of rounds expended increased due to fouled cones, carbon build up on the inside of the barrel and the heat of the barrel. Consequently, the speed dropped from three

---

16. *Detroit Free Press*, June 8, 1863; Bancroft journal, July 1, 1863; Jacobs, "Meteorology of the Battle," pp. 120-21. Eighty-one degrees, in and of itself, is not an uncomfortable temperature; the interpretation of how uncomfortable the day was for the soldiers in reserve, or those engaged in battle, however, was significantly affected by the humidity of the day, which was not recorded but may have been uncomfortable since Gettysburg does not benefit from a breeze over a plain or large body of water. The type of clothing worn, the weight of the armaments and accoutrements, the length of previous days' marches and the heating effect of all the armaments being discharged would have been likely to increase the discomfort of the men.
17. Pfanz, *Gettysburg: The Second Day*, p. 180.

rounds per minute down to two rounds and then down to as low as one round per minute.[18]

The First Division proceeded to the front, advancing along McAllister Mill Road turning west on Granite Schoolhouse Road then left on the Taneytown Road led by the Third Brigade and followed by the Second and First Brigades.[19] The Fifth Corps Ambulance Corps followed the troops with eighty-one wagons. During this advance the Third Brigade was detached to Brig. Gen. Governeur K. Warren and deployed on the slopes of Little Round Top on the extreme left flank of the Union line. As the Third Brigade was detached, the division executed a "by files right" order turn onto the Wheatfield Road. Marching in a column of four, numbering 1,010 men in Sweitzer's brigade and 654 in Col. William S. Tilton's brigade, stretching 400 to 450 yards in length, it took approximately ten minutes for the column of men to reach the point where they would be deployed on the field.[20]

The First Division found that the Third Corps had consolidated parts of its line to meet the challenge at Devil's Den and Rose's Woods. The 40th New York positioned on Stony Hill and, facing northwest, was recalled to the main defensive line beyond Rose's Woods towards Devil's Den and the east branch of Plum Run since they were being "relieved by a portion of the Fifth Corps." Ward's brigade, pivoting on its left flank, repositioned itself in a north/south line at the edge of Rose's Woods to defend against Brig. Gen. George T. Anderson's and Brig. Gen. Henry L. Benning's Confederate Brigades.[21]

The First Division double-quicked up the Wheatfield Road and was personally placed in position by General Sykes along Stony Hill as agreed between himself and General Birney. The brigade, marching west in a column of fours, had to be converted to a battle line facing west as it marched along the Wheatfield Road. This was accomplished by a "right by files into line" command. Sweitzer's brigade was deployed in a brigade battle line whose left, the 32nd Massachusetts, approached the 17th Maine which was posted near the stone wall bordering Rose's Woods near the base of Stony Hill. The warm temperature, double-quick advance and adrenaline pumping through the men's veins must surely have increased the tension

18. OR, vol. 27, pt. 1, p. 592; Houghton journal, July 1, 1863; Paddy Griffith, Battle Tactics of the Civil War (New Haven: Yale University Press, 1987) p. 83.
19. OR, vol. 27, pt. 1, p. 610.
20. Ibid., p. 601; Pfanz, Gettysburg: The Second Day, p. 243.
21. OR, vol. 27, pt. 1, p. 526; Pfanz, Gettysburg: The Second Day, p. 180.

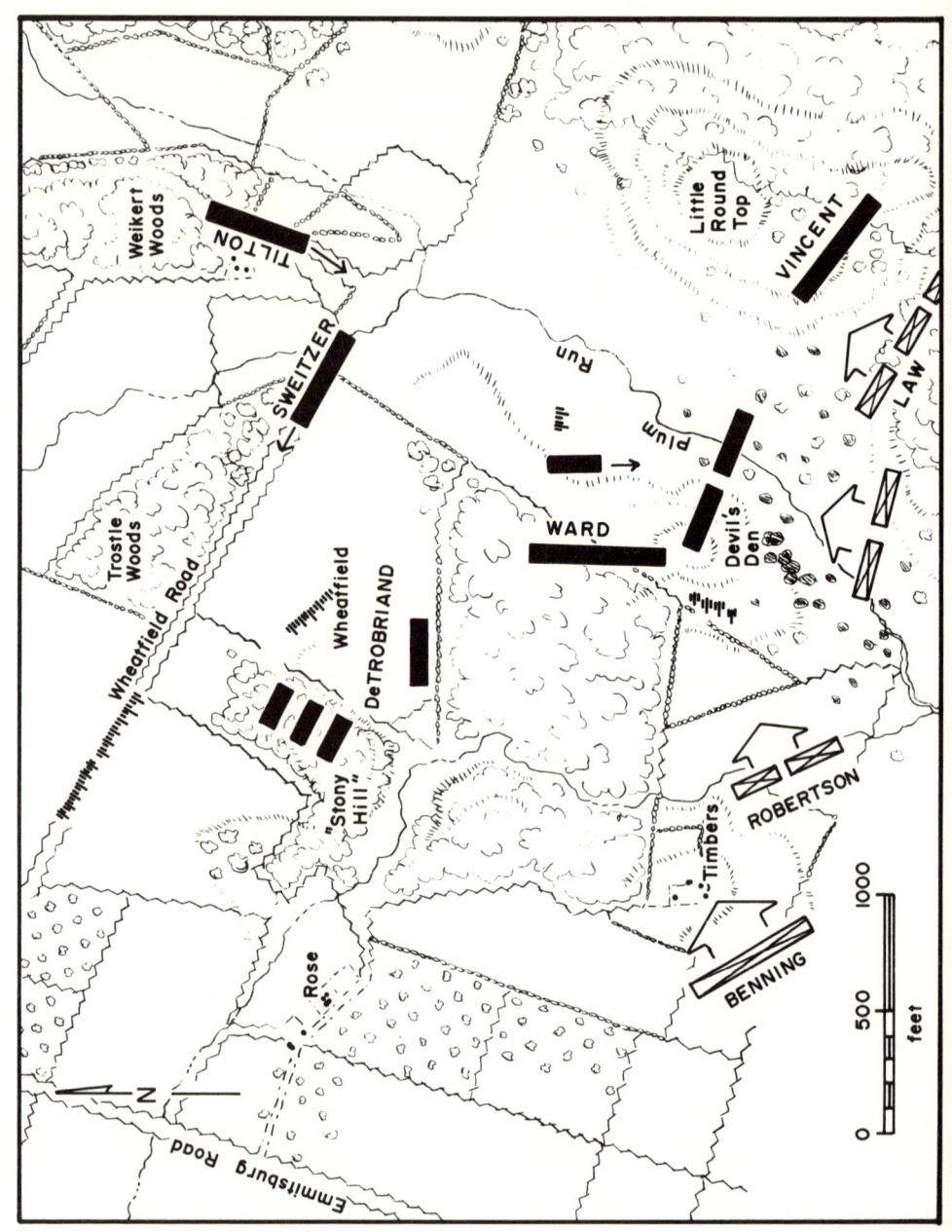

Third Corps redeploys

and apprehension throughout the ranks. Sweitzer's brigade advanced across the Wheatfield, up and over Stony Hill and halted. Tilton's brigade continued beyond Sweitzer's position, wheeled left and deployed facing south, with the 118th Pennsylvania refused and facing west, overlapping and slightly behind de Trobriand's brigade and extending in the direction of the Peach Orchard.[22]

The 32nd Massachusetts, the left of the line, extended too close to de Trobriand's brigade and threatened to be in the line of fire. Colonel Sweitzer therefore ordered the 32nd to change fronts facing south thereby refusing itself on the 62nd Pennsylvania and 4th Michigan.[23] This created an L formation with the 32nd Massachusetts on the left facing south towards Rose's Woods, the 62nd Pennsylvania in the middle and the 4th Michigan on the right both facing west, behind "a ledge of stone 15 to 18 inches in height forming a natural breastwork," anchoring the right flank near the Wheatfield Road.[24]

The battle line formed by the 4th Michigan and 62nd Pennsylvania fell far short from adequately covering the gap to the Wheatfield Road assuming the 32nd Massachusetts' monument is reasonably close to its actual position and that the current National Park Wheatfield Road, then known as Millerstown Road, is reasonably close to the 1863 roadbed. The 32nd Massachusetts, like de Trobriand's brigade, engaged the Confederates of Anderson's division at approximately 5 p.m. Colonel Sweitzer ordered the 62nd Pennsylvania and 4th Michigan to change fronts once again to the south in column. Both regiments were in direct support of the 32nd Massachusetts, which was posted midway down the southern slope of Stony Hill along a 165 foot front. To the left of the 4th Michigan lay a twenty-acre wheatfield its "amber waves of grain" untouched by the ravages of war. It was bordered by the position on the Stony Hill on the west, a stone fence in the east, woods to the south and a road to the north. This unpretentious wheatfield was about to become *the* Wheatfield.[25]

---

22. *OR*, vol. 27, pt. 1, p. 593; *OR Supplement*, vol. 5, p. 191; Pfanz, *Gettysburg: The Second Day*, p. 246. To "refuse" a body of men along a battle line was to change the fighting direction of the subject body of men by ninety degrees to the main battle line. The body of men could be a squad, company or regiment.
23. *OR Supplement*, vol. 5, p. 191.
24. *OR*, vol. 27, pt.1, p. 611; Pfanz, *Gettysburg: The Second Day*, p. 246; John Bancroft to Michigan Adjutant General, July 29, 1863.
25. *OR*, vol. 27, pt.1, p. 611; *OR Supplement*, vol. 5, p. 191; Pfanz, *Gettysburg: The Second Day*, p. 292.

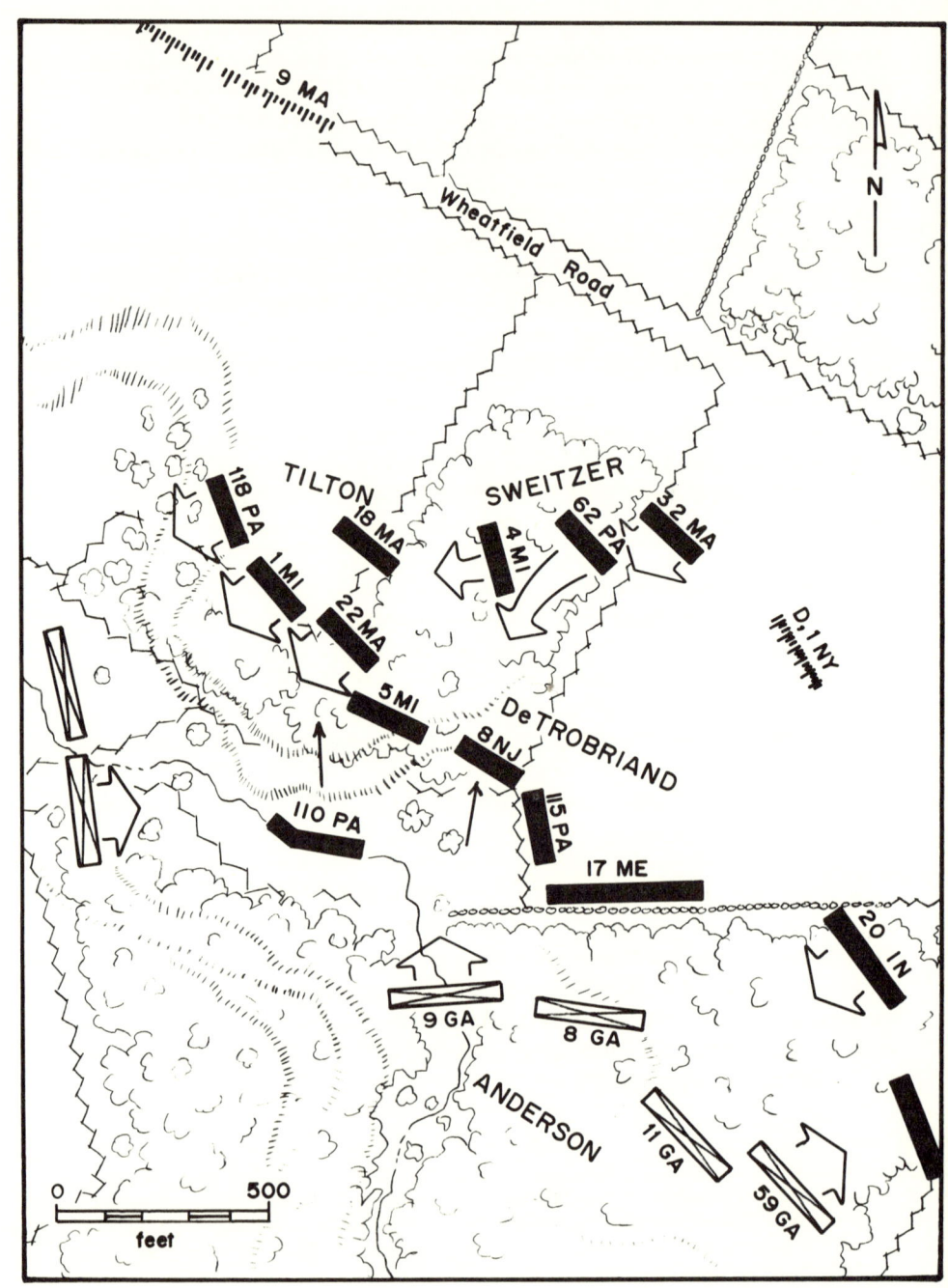

Fifth Corps deploys

Lieutenant Bancroft recorded that when the 4th Michigan took position on Stony Hill, it "found, in the edge of a wood, facing west, a battery in open ground on our right [adjacent to Tilton's 118th Pennsylvania], and part of the Third Corp on our left, facing south, and engaged with the enemy's infantry in the woods to our left [Rose's Woods]." He continued, "There was a battery in the open field in our rear firing over the woods." This was Capt. George B. Winslow's battery of six Napoleons positioned on a rise in the center of the wheatfield providing artillery support over the 17th Maine into Rose's Woods.[26] At this point, James Houghton recalled:

> our officers told us that if any of our canteens were empty that we had better get them filled for we might want water soon. We well understood what that meant so all those that did not have a supply started out in search of water. The ground was quite level and there were no springs to be found. Nearby was a ditch that had some stagnate water in it. We poked the scum [to] one side with our cups then gave the water a spat to scare the bugs and wigglers to the bottom, then filled our canteens and returned to our regiment.[27]

From his vantage point, General Barnes could see a danger in the deployment of his troops that he voiced to General Sykes.[28] The Union defensive line was in a flat based "U" with the infantry on Stony Hill but not fully extended to the Wheatfield Road leaving a gap of about 200 yards, a line of four unsupported field artillery batteries along the Wheatfield Road and Third Corps infantry in the Peach Orchard at the corner of the Wheatfield and Emmitsburg Roads, 300 yards away from the infantry on Stony Hill. General Barnes' concern may have stemmed from the realization that had Vincent's brigade been present bringing the division to full strength, the gap on Stony Hill would have been filled.[29]

The position of General Barnes' troops and the line was deemed vulnerable and perhaps indefensible. He ordered

---

26. *Detroit Free Press*, August 3, 1863, Wyandotte Library, Wyandotte, Michigan; Bancroft journal, July 2, 1863; *OR*, vol. 27, pt. 1, p. 587.
27. Houghton journal, July 2, 1863. The "ditch" that Houghton refers to probably was at the western base of the Wheatfield as it begins the rise up Stony Hill. This section of the Wheatfield is a low, somewhat marshy area extending south to Rose's Woods.
28. *OR*, vol 27, pt 1, p. 601.
29. *Ibid.*, p. 881; Pfanz, *Gettysburg: The Second Day*, pp. 240, 307.

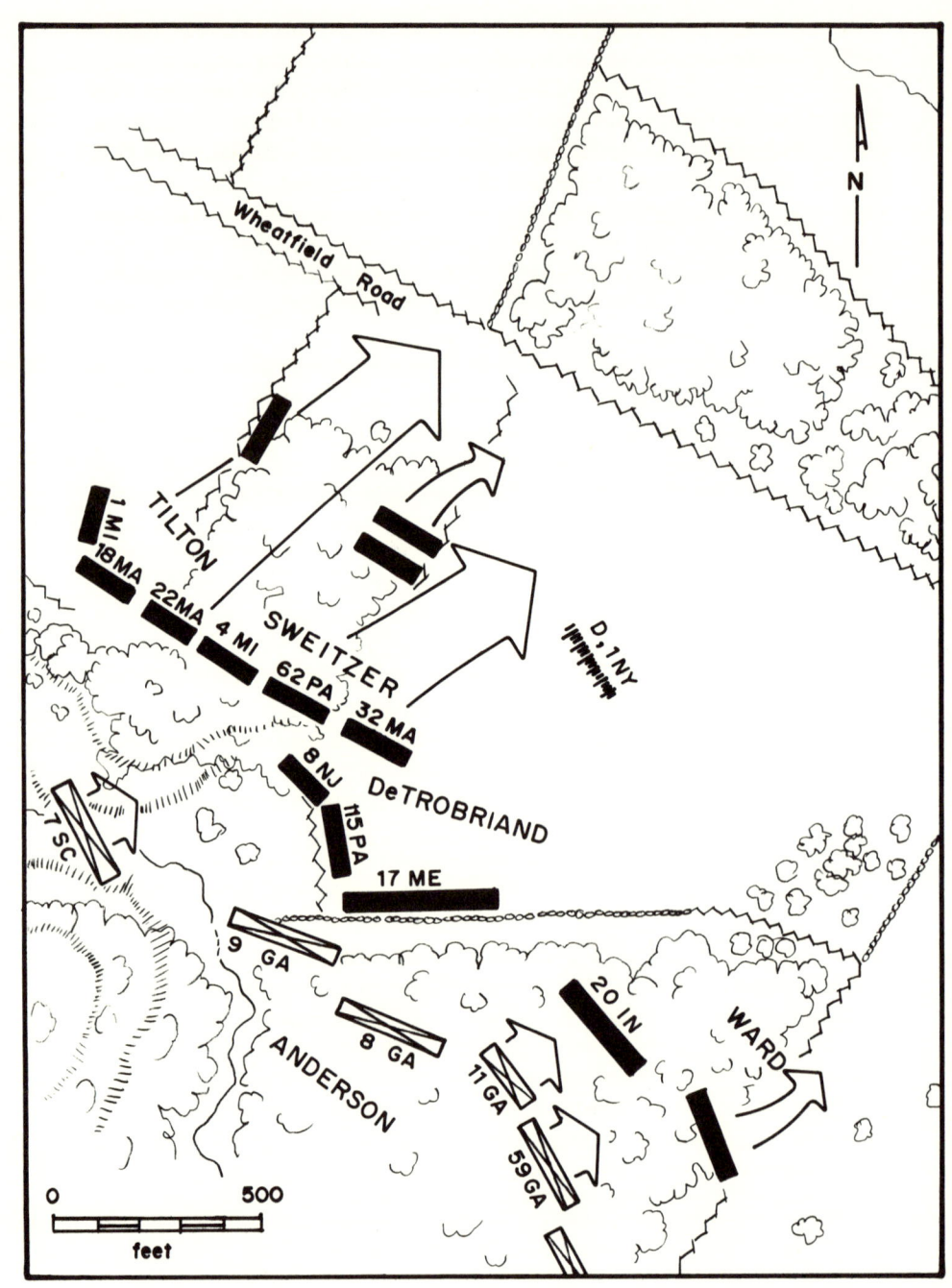

Barnes recalls his troops

Tilton's First Brigade to shift and change fronts to the right; marching north across the Wheatfield Road and re-deployed facing west along the edge of Trostle's Woods, to face the oncoming challenge. Sweitzer's Second Brigade was to fall back beyond the Wheatfield Road into the edge of Trostle's Woods facing south just to the rear of the First Brigade. The division was then in an L shaped formation in and along Trostle's Woods.[30]

Colonel Jeffords recalled his skirmishers and executed General Barnes' order. Lieutenant Bancroft described how the order was affected: "First we faced west, then hinging on the right, swinging backward, we now faced southward, an open wheatfield being between us and the woods, in and beyond which a part of the 3rd Corps were fighting."[31] This description of the movement is believed to be only partially accurate. The change of front and wheel maneuver would have been possible and likely. Where the wheel maneuver ended is in question. Assuming the placement of the 32nd Massachusetts monument along the southern slope of Stony Hill is reasonably accurate, the wheel would have placed the 4th Michigan through the woods of Stony Hill and into the Wheatfield, the Wheatfield Road some 200 yards to the rear. If Lieutenant Bancroft was referring to the 4th's position along Trostle's Woods at the conclusion of the wheel maneuver, then the 32nd Massachusetts would have been significantly behind de Trobriand at the time of Anderson's attack. This does not appear logical, as de Trobriand would have been engulfed at that time and as a supporting unit the 32nd Massachusetts would have been of very little value; yet they were fully engaged during Anderson's attack. More likely, Bancroft's description of the wheel was followed by an about face, forward march in a battle line command to the Wheatfield Road. Lieutenant Bancroft further noted that the regiment was "laying here" pending the receipt of their next set of orders. Considering the Third Corps fighting underway to the 4th's front coupled with wounded streaming through their ranks on the way to the rear, laying on their arms provided some protection from stray and spent bullets and helped preserve the unit's fighting strength.[32]

Orvey Barrett recalled that "the regiment stood under fire at least a half hour before it became engaged, getting a large

---

30. *OR*, vol. 27, pt. 1, pp. 601, 611; Pfanz, *Gettysburg: The Second Day*, p. 272.
31. Bancroft journal, July 2, 1863.
32. *Ibid.*

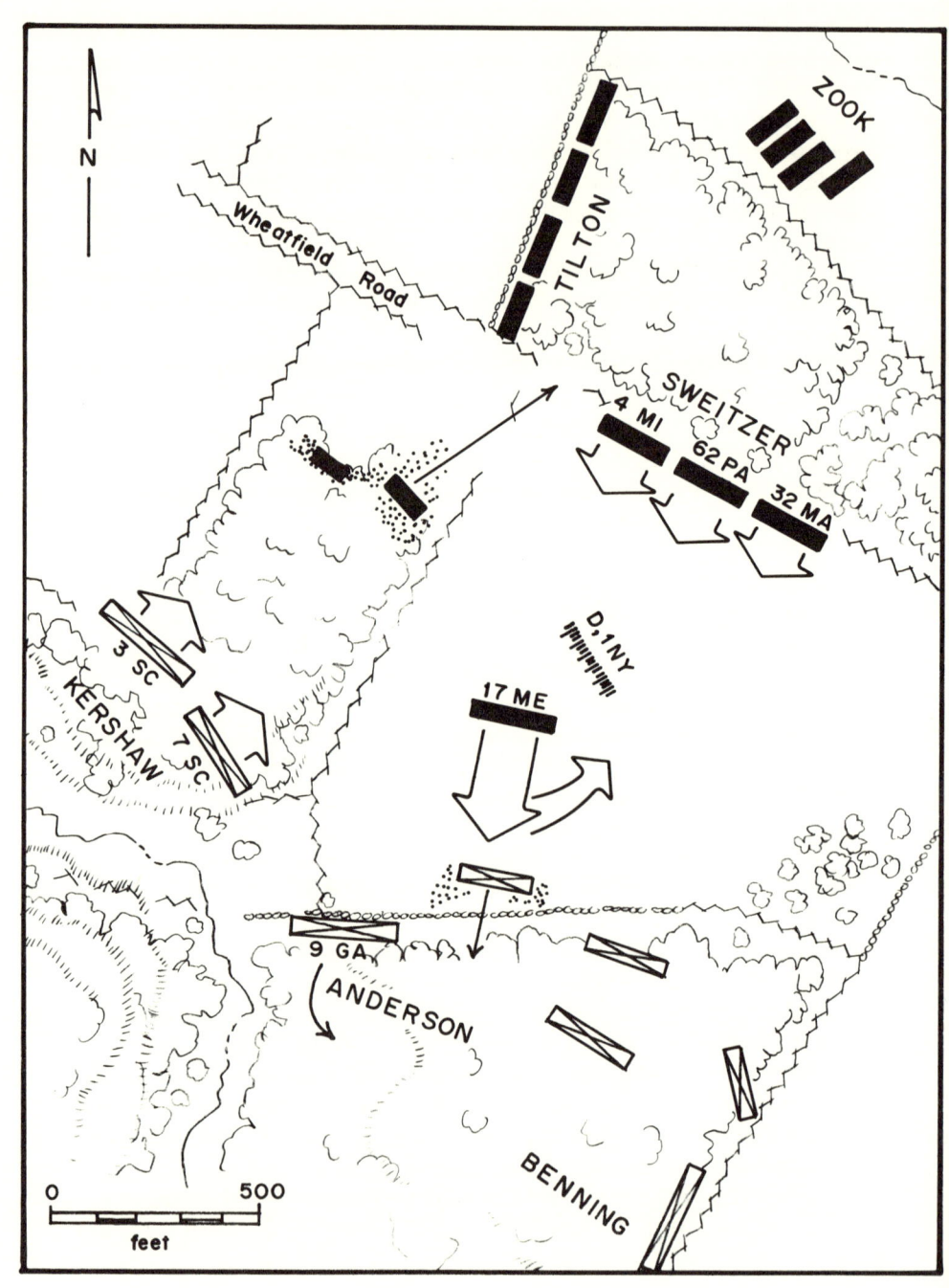

Map by John Heiser

Charge of the 17th Maine

share of spent balls from the front."³³ Jim Houghton recalled this time span somewhat more clearly. Of particular interest is the difference of opinion of the speed of the bullets being received:

> We was now under fire in good earnest. Bullets were whizzing, buzzing and spatting all around us. We were ordered to lie down as we could do no firing while there was other troops in front of us. While we were lying there the man to my left had his blouse sleeve torn from his wrist to his elbow throwing the refuse of his sleeve in my face. Of course we thought this was rather careless work but we could do nothing but lie still and wait. There were frequently wounded men passing by us telling us to go in and give them hell. ³⁴

A good percentage of soldiers of the time were God-fearing men and one can well imagine that as the Second Brigade was deployed in line of battle that afternoon they may have whispered the familiar lines of the 23rd Psalm.

General Barnes' order may have been appropriate in his own judgment; however, it left a huge hole in the Union line that threatened to entrap de Trobriand's brigade, for its right and rear were unprotected. As Brig. Gen. Joseph B. Kershaw's South Carolinians struck the Stony Hill, Anderson's Georgians surged through Rose's Woods once again. De Trobriand went to the rear, expecting to call up reinforcements from the Fifth Corps' First Division but they were leaving the field under General Barnes' orders to a new position 300 yards to the rear.³⁵ Imagine the feeling of frustration and anger that Colonel de Trobriand must surely have experienced. The Confederate brigades of Benning, Anderson and Kershaw continued their drive. Ward's brigade on the left broke, retreated and reformed. The First and Second Brigades of the Fifth Corps had moved to a new position. De Trobriand had essentially three choices: be overrun with heavy casualties, surrender, or retreat and reform. He chose the latter, and pulled back in an orderly fashion over the Stony Hill and through the Wheatfield, halting midway to slow the Confederate advance. De Trobriand reunited his brigade near the Wheatfield Road. The left of Sickles' advanced position had crumbled. The Rebels had cleared the

---

33. Barrett, *Old Fourth Michigan*, p. 22.
34. Houghton journal, July 2, 1863.
35. Pfanz, *Gettysburg: The Second Day*, p. 264; *OR*, vol. 27, pt. 1, p. 520.

Union forces from Devil's Den, Rose's Woods, Stony Hill and the Wheatfield. Ahead laid their goal: Little Round Top, a critical defensive position.[36]

Maj. Gen. Winfield S. Hancock, commanding the Second Corps, saw the situation unfolding from his position on Cemetery Ridge.[37] A messenger rode up requesting a division to come and help. General Hancock ordered Brig. Gen. John Caldwell and his four brigades to march quickly to the Wheatfield. Caldwell's four brigades were commanded by Col. Edward Cross, Brig. Gen. Samuel Zook, Col. Patrick Kelly and Col. John Brooke. The lead brigade, Zook's, advanced from the direction of Trostle's farm and was intercepted by a messenger from General Sickles—Maj. Henry Tremain. General Zook peeled his brigade out of the main column and headed for the western corner of Trostle's Woods. Cross', Kelly's and Brookes' brigades continued on, passed through Trostle's Woods and formed along the eastern edge of Trostle's Woods along the Wheatfield Road.[38] In the western part of the woods confusion was the word of the hour. General Zook's orders were to relieve de Trobriand and close the gap on Stony Hill recently vacated by Tilton's First Brigade and Sweitzer's Second Brigade. Regiments were being organized and deployed in Trostle's Woods in preparation for the advance on Stony Hill. Zook's efforts may have been hampered by the confusion that ensued as Tilton's and Sweitzer's brigades were ordered back from Stony Hill to reform in the same plot of woods. There were then three full brigades in and along a small woods; one brigade was forming to move forward, and two others were reforming having come off Stony Hill. The woods would have been thick with smoke, company officers shouting orders, tree branches falling from cannon shot, wounded from the Third Corps moving to the rear, soldiers checking and clearing cones to reduce the risk of misfires, and noise from the Third Corps fighting in their front.

While General Caldwell's brigades were taking their positions and preparing to advance, General Birney bought them some precious minutes by ordering the 17th Maine and the 5th Michigan, regiments from de Trobriand's brigade, back into the Wheatfield. They advanced midway to the rise of the Wheatfield and commenced firing on Anderson's Georgians who returned to the stone fence bordering Rose's Woods. The maneuver worked. General Zook's brigade advanced into the battle

36. Pfanz, *Gettysburg: The Second Day*, pp. 264, 262.
37. *Ibid.*, p. 268.
38. Eric Campbell, "Caldwell Clears the Wheatfield," *Gettysburg Magazine*, no. 3 (July 1990): p. 33; Pfanz, *Gettysburg: The Second Day*, p. 269-270.

relieving de Trobriand "when our ammunition was just exhausted."[39] Zook, on horseback, led his brigade out of Trostle's Woods, across the Wheatfield Road through the northwestern corner of the Wheatfield and onto Stony Hill to engage Kershaw's South Carolinians. General Zook, riding high in his saddle was a marvelous target; a minie ball struck home. Colonel Cross and his brigade marched straight across the eastern edge of the Wheatfield with "his left resting on the woods which skirted the field" and engaged Anderson's brigade. He went to his extreme left to coordinate a flanking charge on the Georgians. Colonel Cross received a mortal wound. Kelly's Irish Brigade filled the gap in the Wheatfield between Cross on the left and Zook on the right. Kelly's brigade advanced on a diagonal towards Stony Hill, their target being a gap between the left of Anderson's Georgians and the right of Kershaw's South Carolinians. Kershaw rode to Brig. Gen. Paul J. Semmes and to the 15th South Carolina for reinforcements then returned to his brigade. Kelly's Irish Brigade opened fire at 200 yards just as Zook's brigade resumed its attack.[40] The flanks of the two Union brigades met and overlapped on the slope of Stony Hill. Fighting once again became fierce with men rushing and lead flying. The Union was beginning to carry the day as Kershaw's brigade crumbled; some surrendered and the majority started to fall back towards Rose's Farm. Brig. Gen. William T. Wofford's fresh brigade of Georgians came to the rescue and the Confederate attack upon the Union was renewed with vigor toward Zook's brigade on Stony Hill and Tilton's brigade along the western edge of Trostle's Woods. While this action was taking place, Caldwell's Fourth Brigade, Brooke's, entered the fray by marching diagonally across the Wheatfield toward the southwest corner of the field where it swept Anderson's Georgians from the northern edge of Rose's Woods.[41]

The Union now held a line from Trostle's Woods across Stony Hill to the northern edge of Rose's Woods. The left of this line had become tenuous at best, for Brooke's brigade was now receiving fire from multiple directions and from General Semmes' brigade which had moved up to reinforce Anderson's brigade.

General Caldwell's Second Corps troops were hotly engaged at Rose's Woods and on a north/south line along Stony Hill. General Caldwell was of the opinion he was about to turn the

---

39. *Ibid.*, pp. 265-66; *OR*, vol. 27, pt.1, p. 520.
40. *Ibid.*, pp. 277, 379; *Ibid.*, pt. 2, p. 368; Pfanz, *Gettysburg: The Second Day*, p. 272.
41. Pfanz, *Gettysburg: The Second Day*, p. 243; *OR*, vol. 27, pt. 2, p. 369.

Rebel attack but needed reinforcements for the final push. He rode to Colonel Sweitzer and requested the Second Brigade. Colonel Sweitzer replied he would advance, but the order must come from General Barnes. General Caldwell rode to General Barnes, repeated his request and gained authorization to proceed.[42]

> The combat deepens, on, ye braves,
> Who rush to glory or the grave!
> Wave, Michigan! all thy banners wave,
> And charge with all thy chivalry![43]

Colonel Sweitzer ordered his 1,010 men to rise and prepare to advance across the Wheatfield. As a prelude to the advance, Colonel Sweitzer recounted, "General Barnes got out in front of them, and made a few patriotic remarks, to which they responded with a cheer." The color guard stepped six paces out in front of the line and led the way. To his right was Zook's brigade along Stony Hill protecting the right flank of Sweitzer's brigade. The brigade advanced "giving cheers" with the 32nd Massachusetts on the left, the 62nd Pennsylvania in the center and the 4th Michigan on the right with its extreme right on the edge of the woods along Stony Hill. As the brigade advanced, First Lieutenant and Chief Ambulance Officer of the First Division, Joseph C. Ayer, placed his stretcher bearers behind the troops and his ambulance train 200 yards to the rear.[44] The 4th Michigan's battle line was arrayed by company, from left to right, as follows: B, G, K, E, H, C, I, D, F and A. As the regiment halted and prepared to fire, the color guard returned to the battle line. John Bancroft wrote that the regiment "advanced thirty rods and commenced firing to the front with nothing on our flank. A few skirmishers had been there but returned before we advanced."[45] The brigade resumed its march approximately 350 yards to the point previously occupied by the 17th Maine and the 5th Michigan who had retreated toward Little Round Top. John Bancroft continued: "Those of the Third Corps were falling back as we advanced and passed through our ranks just as we began firing." Jim Houghton recalled, "at this moment the Rebels ceased firing and there was a lull in the battle.

---

42. *Ibid.*, pt. 1, pp. 379, 602, 611; Pfanz, *Gettysburg: The Second Day*, p. 290.
43. *Michigan in the War*, p. 174.
44. *OR*, vol. 27, pt. 1, p. 602, 611; Pfanz, *Gettysburg: The Second Day*, p. 290; *OR*, vol. 27, pt. 1, pp. 597, 606.
45. Bancroft journal, July 2, 1863.

... After waiting here a few minutes," the brigade continued its march, at right shoulder shift, behind waving battle flags to the stone fence separating the Wheatfield from Rose's Woods and then the 4th Michigan continued "beyond the stone fence" into Rose's Woods where it was "most exposed." At this point they became engaged with the 9th Georgia forty yards in their front who were laying along the gentle bank of the southern branch of Plum Run. Company I lost its top two non-commissioned officers at that point in the engagement: twenty-one-year-old First Sgt. John H. Kydd and twenty-two-year-old Sgt. William H. Jackson. Both men were combat-tested veterans who had entered Company I as privates on June 20, 1861.[46]

Colonel Sweitzer reported that he immediately noticed regiments leaving the woods on the right which he assumed to be Union troops being relieved. Colonel Sweitzer wrote that sounds of musketry fire were coming from the woods in their rear. He initially assumed it was from Union troops firing over the Second Brigade. Brigade headquarters flag color-bearer Edward Martin commented to Colonel Sweitzer; "Colonel, I'll be _____ if I don't think we are faced the wrong way; the Rebs are up there in the woods behind us, on the right." The Union troops Colonel Sweitzer observed were none other than Generals Zook, Kelly and Brooke's brigades pulling back from the onslaught of Kershaw's South Carolinians, and Wofford's and Semmes' Georgians. Sweitzer soon received word from both the 4th Michigan and 62nd Pennsylvania that confirmed his color-bearer's observation. Sweitzer executed two orders. First he ordered Lt. John Seitz, his aide-de-camp, to ride in search of General Barnes to seek the General's orders and observe the Rebel's position. Second, he ordered the 62nd Pennsylvania and 4th Michigan to change fronts to the right to meet the challenge.[47]

The Rebels continued to close the noose around the 4th Michigan. Colonel Jeffords executed an extraordinary maneuver while changing fronts towards the on-rushing wave of gray clad men. Colonel Jeffords ordered what best could be described as a wheel about the center of his regiment by pulling the left forward and the right backwards into a battle line facing west. Such an order demonstrates the discipline of his line officers and non-commisioned officers and to the training of the troops. The supposition of this maneuver is supported in a letter

46. Houghton journal, July 2, 1863; *OR*, vol. 27, pt. 1, p. 611; Pfanz, *Gettysburg: The Second Day*, p. 295; *Detroit Free Press*, August 3, 1863.
47. *OR*, vol. 27, pt. 1, p. 612; Pfanz, *Gettysburg: The Second Day*, pp. 291, 293.

written after the war by Henry S. Seage. In it he writes: "Col. Jeffords gave the order for the left of the regiment to pivot on the line while the right should swing back into the wheat-field and so form a new line, while in the act of this movement we became mixed up with the Rebs."[48] Lieutenant Colonel Lumbard on the extreme right saw the danger at the same time and issued orders complimentary to Colonel Jefford's orders to change fronts. "Lieut. Col. Lombard [sic], on the right, discovering the rebels advancing in line of battle behind our right flank, ordered the right to swing around or change front, then to fall back slowly, as they were upon and had broken the right companies."[49] The maneuver was noteworthy but not wholly successful since it was probably not fully executed, for Kershaw's and Wofford's brigades hit the right flank hard, bending then breaking the flank and sending confusion surging through the line. Meanwhile, Lieutenant Seitz returned to Colonel Sweitzer, on foot as his horse was shot out from under him, and reported that he could not find General Barnes and that the Rebels were in the woods as far back as where the advance started and along the road rear of the Wheatfield.[50] The noose had tightened quickly.

James Houghton recorded:

> We moved up in line of battle to the south end of this narrow strip of woods that lies west of the wheatfield [Stony Hill]. Here we opened fire on the Rebs in good earnest. We were busily engaged firing at the Rebs that was south of us when the rattling of canteens and a heavy tread of infantry was heard in our rear. Observing a little closer we saw that they wore the gray uniform and was not over 10 rods distant [75 yards]. They were on the double quick passing through the woods out into the wheatfield east of us. Our good old regiment was now in a critical situation; there was Rebels southwest, north and northeast of us. There was now only two things for us to do; that was to surrender or pass out directly in front of their lines and receive the contents of their well loaded rifles. Soon the order came to about face forward double quick march. In less then two minutes our Regiment was passing out across

---

48. Henry Seage to John Bachelder, September 23, 1884, in David L. and Audrey J. Ladd, *The Bachelder Papers: Gettysburg in Their Own Words* (Dayton, Ohio: Morningside, 1994-95), 2: 1070-1073.
49. *Detroit Free Press*, August 3, 1863.
50. *OR*, vol. 27, pt. 1, p. 612.

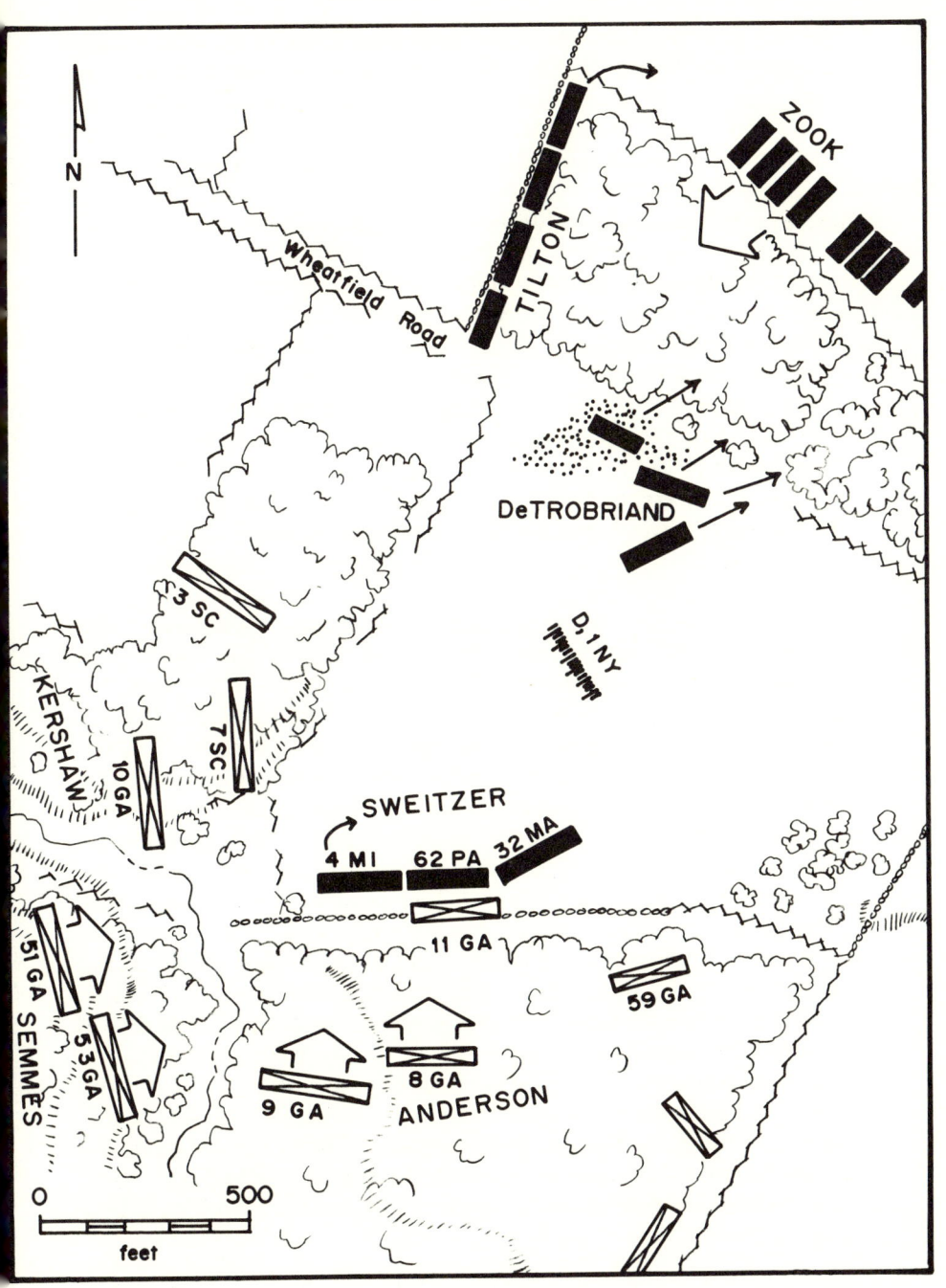

Sweitzer changes fronts

the wheatfield directly in front of the Rebels. It was here that the crash came. A storm of lead swept through our ranks like hail. Many of our noble boys fell to the ground never to rise to their feet again, others were wounded but could hobble away.[51]

Lieutenant Bancroft added his perspective:

> The Rebels had silenced the battery on the right which was at a considerable distance, had taken the pieces and were advancing upon our flank. We moved across the wheatfield and opened fire in response to the stray shots that were coming from the Rebels in our front while the force approaching on our flank came in collision with the right of the regiment in the woods by which they were checked in part, but their extreme left continued to advance so that they were upon all sides of us.[52]

The 4th's color guard, particularly Thomas Tarnsney the color-bearer, became a focal point of desperate fighting.[53] Bancroft recorded on July 29, "We fell back toward the east, in tolerable order, the right of the regiment being mostly taken prisoners, and the left following the Sixty-Second on our left, leaving a small squad near our colors, while the brigade color was followed by a squad of our men. . . . The rebels came in with yells, and we fell back rapidly. There was little cover, and many were wounded."[54] The 4th's color-bearer, proudly holding a new flag not more than 120 days old, lost possession of it. Colonel Jeffords, who at the time he took possession of the new flag swore his allegiance and vowed not to let it fall into enemy hands, saw the flag in the hands of a Confederate. Calling to fellow officers Second Lt. R. Watson Seage, First Lt. Michael Vreeland and Maj. Jarius W. Hall to follow, he rushed to retrieve the flag. Colonel Jeffords grabbed it with his left hand as Lieutenant Seage struck the Confederate with his sword, dropping the man. Instantly, Colonel Jeffords was shot in the leg and "thrust through with a bayonet [in the side of the chest] in a contest over his colors."[55] Major Hall, revolver in hand, shot

51. Houghton journal, July 2, 1863.
52. John Bancroft to Michigan Adjutant General, December 22, 1863, Heckert Collection.
53. As the brigade retreated diagonally across the Wheatfield, the 4th Michigan's battle line was in disarray.
54. *Detroit Free Press*, August 3, 1863.
55. *OR*, vol. 27, pp. 602, 612.

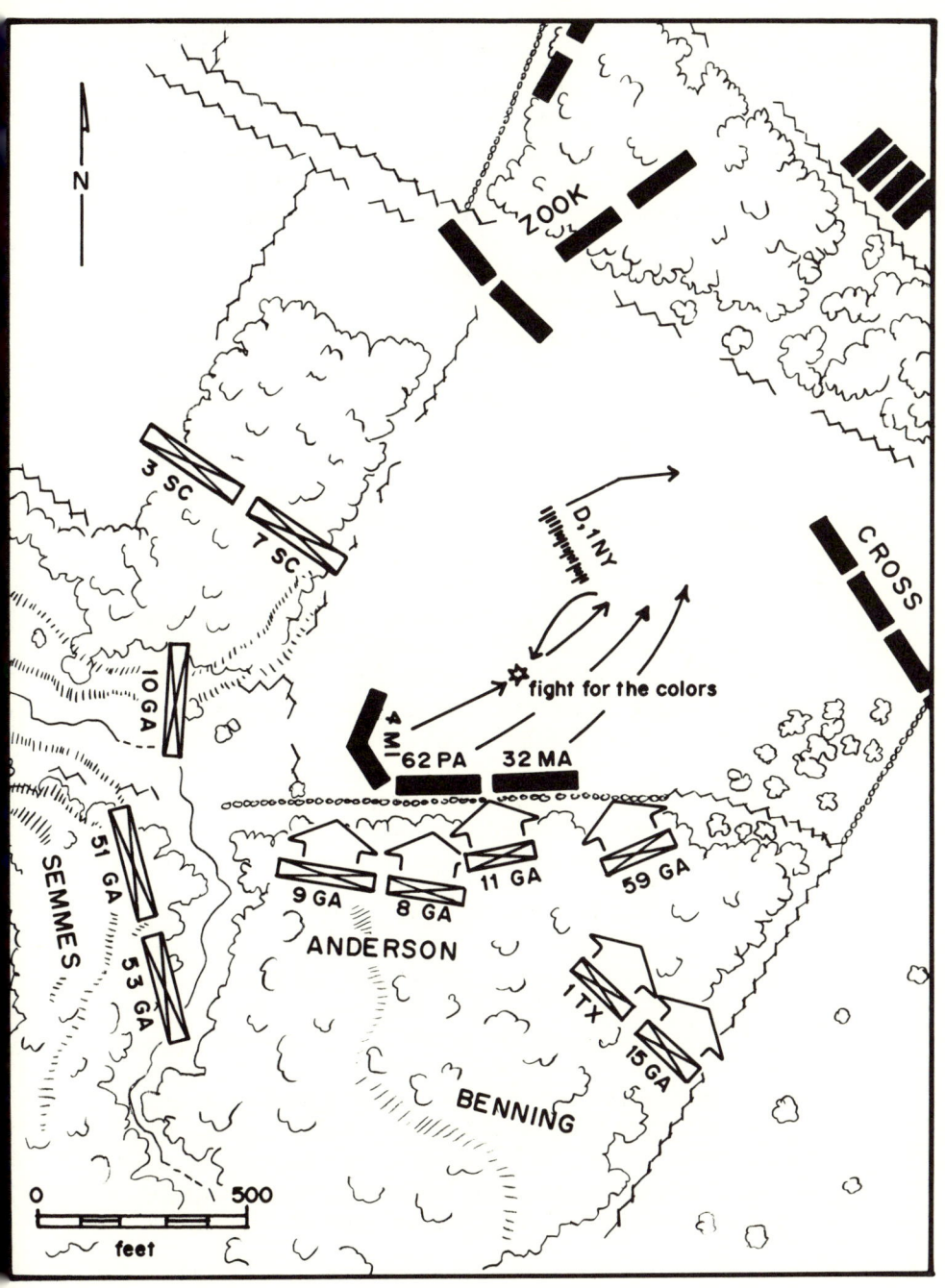

Map by John Heiser

Sweitzer retreats

the Confederate who had bayoneted the colonel. Colonel Jeffords, mortally wounded and without his flag, was carried off the field by his men. "He lived in a semi-delirious condition for a short time" reported First Lt. and Quartermaster Robert Campbell, and died the next day. "But our flag was lost," Campbell continued, "said to have been torn to pieces in the general melee."[56] Henry Seage recalled the incident in a post-war letter:

> Col. Jeffords seeing our colors in possession of the Reb's [sic] called on my brother who was adjutant of the regiment to rescue the colors. Those three made a dash for the colors. The colonel secured the colors or at least had his left hand on the staff when my brother made a swinging cut at the Reb (who had the staff in his left hand) striking him in the neck; killing him instantly. In the fight the colors were torn in shreds (what little remained). By this time these three were surrounded by Rebs, and in the act of fighting their way out, Col. Jeffords was killed, by bayonet thrust through the body. My brother was shot through both breasts and bayoneted in the left leg. Lt. Vreeland was shot through the left breast and right arm and scalp wounded by clubbed musket. These three fell as they fought, side by side.[57]

Command then passed to Lt. Col. George W. Lumbard.

From the Vreeland family papers comes a description of Lieutenant Vreeland's fight for his life:

> Lieutenant Vreeland became aware of the direction of the new attack when he was struck by a bullet which passed through his right lung from back to front. Unable to shout a warning to his men as his throat filled with blood, he tried to indicate with his sword the direction of the new danger. As he raised his arm he was struck by a second bullet which shattered his right hand and knocked him down. Assailed on all sides, his company, now reduced to 23 men was wiped out; all killed, wounded or captured. As Lieutenant Vreeland lay helpless on the ground a Confederate soldier moved

---

56. Campbell, "Pioneer Memories," p. 571.
57. Henry Seage to John Bachelder, September 23, 1884, in Ladd, *Bachelder Papers*, pp. 1070-73.

Michigan Historical Collection, University of Michigan

Jarius W. Hall

Jarius W. Hall, from Washtenaw County, received his commission on May 16, 1861, as second lieutenant of Company D at the age of twenty-one. He was mustered into service at Adrian on June 20, 1861. He rose to the rank of lieutenant colonel during the first enlistment period of the 4th. He accepted the position of colonel of the Reorganized 4th and rose to the rank of brevet brigadier general of United States Volunteers on March 13, 1865. Hall, a major at Gettysburg, is the officer who shot the Confederate soldier who bayoneted Colonel Jeffords.

to finish him with a bayonet, but was ordered away by one of his own officers.[58]

There is some confusion as to who shot the Rebel who first captured the 4th's flag. One position is that Colonel Jeffords shot the Rebel with his pistol before being bayoneted. The marker in the Wheatfield commemorating the struggle follows this line of thought. In actuality, however, Colonel Jeffords had given his pistol to Quartermaster Robert Campbell late in June. Robert Campbell recalled the incident:

> Colonel Jeffords came to me and said, "I see that a large number of the men in the regiment have taken to wearing hats. Of course they are much more comfortable than caps in the hot weather, but it isn't soldierlike and I want you to draw caps for the men." Jeffords and I had been schoolmates together at the high school, several years before and had not met since then until here in the army. When he spoke about drawing the caps, I said to him, "It is for the company commanders to call for caps for their men in their requisition to me. Then I will make requisition for them in bulk through the proper channels. . . . Well," he said, "I order you to get a cap for every man in the regiment who hasn't one without company requisitions." I smiled in his face at the new departure and said, "All right, Colonel, but you must give me a definite written order before I can do it." He went back to his quarters, and in the course of about ten minutes returned. "Quartermaster," said he, "you needn't send for the caps. But I want to make you a present. I was at the first Bull Run battle, on the Peninsula, in the Seven Days fight in front of Richmond, Second Bull Run, Antietam, Fredericksburg and Chancellorsville." Then putting his hand in his pocket he drew out a large six-shot, self-cocking revolver. "In all these campaigns," said he, "I have never needed to use this and it has been a heavy load to carry. You as quartermaster are liable to be mixed up with guerrillas and have much more need of it then I have, and beside you have much better means of transportation for heavy artillery." As the occasion was half-serious, half-comic one, I took the weapon and made a corresponding

---

58. Cecile Vreeland Collection, Waldport, Oregon.

Cecile Vreeland Collection

Michael J. Vreeland

Michael J. Vreeland entered the service in Adrian on June 20, 1861, at the age of twenty-two as sergeant of Company I. He rose through the ranks receiving promotions to first sergeant, second lieutenant of Company D, first lieutenant of Company D, first lieutenant of Company I. He was wounded at Gettysburg and mustered out in Detroit on June 30, 1864, at the expiration of his enlistment. He re-entered the service as captain of Company D of the Reorganized 4th. He continued his rise in the military obtaining the ranks of lieutenant colonel, brevet colonel and brigadier general of United States Volunteers "for gallant and meritorious services during the war." He was mustered out of service in Houston, Texas, on May 26, 1866.

sophomoric speech in reply. This was my last interview, with Colonel Jeffords. . . . Still have it as a relic.[59]

Colonel Sweitzer ordered a retreat and fire, diagonally across the Wheatfield to the northeast corner closest to Little Round Top as best as possible since brigade and regimental order had begun to fail. Lieutenant Bancroft stated they "ordered us to wheel to the rear, to face them and then fall back slowly across the wheatfield to form again."[60] The 4th Michigan, standing in a field of chest-high wheat, with Rebels in its front, right and rear, found itself in disorder and in hand-to-hand combat.

The Second Brigade was in a full scale withdrawal with the troops of opposing forces intermingled. General Kershaw reported that "the whole of my left wing advanced to the charge, sweeping the enemy before them, without a moment's stand, across the stone wall, beyond the wheat-field, up the foot of the mountain."[61] Bancroft recalled "We broke crossing the wheatfield, many men never left the woods and were taken prisoner."[62] The 4th Michigan's flag had been captured introducing yet more confusion into the ranks. The flag was normally a rallying point. Upon whose flag should they rally to exit the field of battle? Some of the 4th rallied with the 62nd Pennsylvania flag and some around the brigade flag. With these banners leading the way, they crossed the stone fence at the northeast end of the Wheatfield and continued on, passed through the ranks of the Pennsylvania Reserves who rose up, fired a volley into the pursuing Rebels then pressed a successful counterconcharge against the Confederates, driving them from the Wheatfield. Jim Houghton recalled the wounding of his captain during the retreat: "Our Captain James B. McLean was wounded in the shin of the left leg and heel but could yet hobble along. He asked me to aid him in getting to the hospital. I told him that I would do what I could for him. I carried all of his things even his sword and belt. He said his sword hurt the wound on his leg."[63] The 4th Michigan continued on through the ranks of the Pennsylvania Reserves and rallied around Lieutenant Colonel Lumbard by First Lt. Aaron F. Walcott's 3rd Battery, Massachusetts Light Artillery. The regiment reformed

59. Campbell, "Pioneer Memories," p. 570.
60. *OR*, vol. 27, pt. 1, p. 612; John Bancroft to Michigan Adjutant General, December 22, 1863, Heckert Collection.
61. *OR*, vol. 27, pt. 2, p. 369.
62. John Bancroft letter to Michigan Adjutant General, July 29, 1863.
63. *OR*, vol. 27, pt. 1, p. 612; Houghton journal, July 2, 1863.

Steve Roberts Collection

Richard Watson Seage

Richard Watson Seage, eldest son of Chaplain Seage, enlisted in Company E as corporal on June 20, 1861, at the age of twenty-three. He was promoted to sergeant and was commissioned second lieutenant of Company I on April 1, 1863. He was wounded at Malvern Hill and wounded severely at the Wheatfield, resulting in a disability discharge on December 31, 1863. Not content to remain at home, he re-entered the service as regimental quartermaster for the Reorganized 4th. He was discharged March 6, 1865, holding the rank of brevet captain of United States Volunteers.

and moved in an orderly fashion to the rear to an open field behind the Weikert Farm. "Darkness closed the fight and we spent the night in gathering the wounded" recorded John Bancroft. The regiment came out with about 55 men but grew to a roll call of 88 by morning and continued to grow to 139 by the following day.[64] For the 4th Michigan Volunteer Infantry, as well as for the rest of those who fought there, that little twenty-acre plot of wheat had now become *the* Wheatfield.

---

64. John Bancroft letter to Michigan Adjutant General, December 22, 1863, Heckert Collection; *OR*, vol. 27, pt. 1, p. 613.

Monroe County Historical Society

Unidentified members of the 4th Michigan
A group of members of Company D. Note that three soldiers are wearing fez caps: a knitted stocking type cap with a tassel, sometimes referred to as a Canadian cap. This suggests that the photograph was taken during the early war period. Jonas Richardson is believed to be the soldier not wearing a jacket.

Monroe County Historical Society

Unidentified members of the 4th Michigan

A group of members of Company D including an officer. As in the previous photograph, several soldiers are wearing fez caps, suggesting this was an early war photograph. The officer could be either Capt. John Randolf or First Lt. Richard De Puy.

Michigan Historical Collection, University of Michigan
Unidentified members of the 4th Michigan
This photograph is of members of Company D. The names of the officers are unknown. The photograph appears to be from the early war years.

National Archives

Unidentified members of the 4th Michigan

This photograph is from early in the war. Note that the men are wearing fez caps and that there is a Sibley tent in the background. Sibley tents were more common in the early war years than in later war years.

Dale Niesen collection

Unidentified member of the 4th Michigan

An unidentified infantryman of the 4th Michigan. The soldier is wearing a fez cap, suggesting the photograph was taken in the early war years.

Monroe County Historical Society

Unidentified member of the 4th Michigan

The photograph is of an unidentified infantryman of the 4th Michigan. The soldier is wearing a fez cap, suggesting the photograph was taken in the early war years. Note also that his pants are either gray or very light blue, also suggesting early war years. A cartridge box sling is over his right shoulder thereby resting on his left hip and it is lacking the eagle breast plate. This also suggests an early war photograph.

Michigan State Archives

Unidentified members of the 4th Michigan
Unidentified members of the 4th taken early in the war, possibly at Adrian. Note the basket of apples on the left, the suitcase on the right and the civilian shoes being worn. The man in the center and in the tent is holding a D handled knife or sword.

Michigan State Archives
Unidentified members of the 4th Michigan
Unidentified members of the 4th taken early in the war. Note the squirrel sitting on the left leg of the soldier in the center of the photograph and the short sword stuck in the waistbelt of the soldier on the right side of the picture.

National Archives

Unidentified member of the 4th Michigan
An unidentified corporal of the 4th. Of particular interest are the two side arms stuck in his waistbelt.

Michigan State Archives
Unidentified members of the 4th Michigan
Unidentified members of the 4th. Four of the soldiers are wearing fez caps, suggesting an early war photograph.

Monroe County Historical Society
Unidentified member of the 4th Michigan
An unidentified member of Company D. Note the side arm stuck in the soldier's waist belt and the fixed bayonet. Side arms were not normally carried by privates.

National Archives
Richard Cramer
Richard Cramer enlisted in Company I on June 20, 1861 at the age of eighteen. He was discharged on disability before the Gettysburg campaign on February 16, 1863.

Monroe County Historical Society

Adelbert F. Day

Adelbert F. Day was mustered into the service of Company B in Adrian on June 20, 1861, at the age of eighteen. He was captured at Gettysburg and returned to the regiment at Culpepper, Virginia, on October 6, 1863. Day re-enlisted and served until his discharge in Detroit on September 11, 1865.

Dale Niesen collection

Samuel De Golyer

Samuel De Golyer received his commission as captain of Company F on May 16, 1861, at the age of thirty-three. He was mustered into service at Adrian on June 20, 1861. He resigned on January 13, 1862, having held the rank of major since September 25, 1861. He re-entered the service as captain of Battery H, 1st Light Artillery on March 11, 1862. De Golyer died on August 8, 1863 from wounds received on May 28, 1863, at Vicksburg, Mississippi.

Dearborn Historical Museum

Josiah D. Emerson

Josiah Emerson, of Hillsdale County, was twenty-one when he enlisted as Company E's sergeant on June 20, 1861. He was wounded at Gaines' Mill in 1862 and again at Laurel Hill in 1864. He rose to the rank of first lieutenant on December 31, 1862, and held that rank until his discharge at the end of his term of service on June 30, 1864.

Hudson Historical Museum

Luther C. French

Luther French, of Hudson, Michigan, entered the service on August 23, 1862, as assistant surgeon. He was commissioned as surgeon in March 1863. He was discharged on disability on May 21, 1863, just six weeks before the battle at Gettysburg.

Monroe County Historical Society

Henry A. Grannis

Henry A. Grannis, of Lenawee County, was thirty-three when he accepted his commission on May 16, 1861, as first lieutenant of Company C. In addition, he was commissioned quartermaster on the same date. He was mustered into service at Adrian on June 20, 1861. Grannis served as acting division quartermaster from January to October, 1862, after which time he was promoted to captain of Company F. He resigned and was honorably discharged on November 6, 1862.

Monroe Historical Society

David D. Marshall

David D. Marshall, of Lenawee County, entered the service at the age of thirty-four as captain of Company G, having received his commission on May 16, 1861, and mustered in at Adrian on June 20, 1861. He was mustered out in Detroit on June 30, 1864, at the expiration of his enlistment. He re-entered the service as captain of Company D of the 13th Infantry on November 28, 1864, and was mustered out in Detroit on June 30, 1865.

Monroe County Historical Society
Ezra Brown

Mr. Brown, of Clinton County, entered the service in Adrian on June 20, 1861 at the age of 22 as a private in Company K. By August 4, 1861 he was a corporal of the same company. He was promoted to Sergeant on July 1, 1862 and just one year and one day later he was wounded in The Wheatfield. He was mustered out in Detroit on June 28, 1864 at the expiration of his enlistment.

National Archives

Senter S. Parker

Senter S. Parker, the officer on the right, of Monroe, Michigan, entered the service in Adrian on June 20, 1861, at the age of twenty-two as sergeant of Company H. He was assigned as the regimental commissary sergeant on September 1, 1861. He re-enlisted and was commissioned second lieutenant of Company B on July 26, 1864. He resigned on January 31, 1865. This photograph was taken sometime in 1864 as he is wearing officer's bars. Of special note is the black man in the photograph, a runaway slave that stayed with the 4th Michigan until arrangements could be made for him to settle in Michigan.

Monroe County Historical Society

William H. Plummer

William H. Plummer, of Washtenaw County, entered the service in Adrian on June 20, 1861, at the age of twenty-one as a private in Company G. He held the rank of corporal at the time of his discharge in Detroit on June 30, 1864, at the expiration of his enlistment. Plummer was wounded at Gettysburg.

Dale Niesen collection

Simon B. Preston

Simon B. Preston, of Hudson, Michigan, received his commission at the age of thirty-five on May 16, 1861, as first lieutenant of Company F. He was mustered into service at Adrian on June 20, 1861. First Lieutenant Preston was taken prisoner on July 21, 1861, and subsequently returned to the regiment. He was wounded at Gaines' Mill, Virginia on June 27, 1862, and died three days later.

Michigan Historical Collection, University of Michigan
Jonas D. Richardson

Jonas D. Richardson, of Washtenaw County, enlisted in Company D as corporal at the age of twenty-one in Adrian on June 20, 1861. He rose to the rank of sergeant. He was transferred to the Invalid Corps on September 30, 1863. Note the piping on his frock coat and knee-high boots, both of which are unusual. Note also that the photograph was taken in a studio.

Michigan Historical Collection, University of Michigan
Jonas Richardson
Jonas Richardson in a post-war photograph.

Hudson Historical Museum

Morris P. Severance

Morris Severance, of Lenawee County, enlisted in Company F on June 20, 1861, at the age of twenty-one. He was wounded on June 26, 1862, and subsequently discharged on disability at Harrison's Landing, Virginia, on October 16, 1862. The woman in the photograph is his wife, Adelia Severance.

Dale Niesen collection

Joseph L. Smith

Joseph L. Smith, of Hudson, Michigan, received his commission at the age of thirty-one on May 16, 1861, as second lieutenant of Company F. He was wounded at Gaines' Mill, Virginia on June 27, 1862, and suffered the amputation of a leg. He resigned and was honorably discharged on March 7, 1863. Of particular note in the photograph is the gray color of his uniform. Some state militia units wore gray before the war, and the 4th Michigan wore gray when they left Michigan bound for Washington.

Dale Niesen collection

Edgar C. Stoddard

Edgar C. Stoddard responded to the call for volunteers and enlisted in Company A at the age of nineteen. He was mustered into service at Adrian on June 20, 1861. He was discharged three months later on September 1, 1861.

Monroe County Historical Society

Joseph N. Totten

Joseph N. Totten, of Monroe County, was mustered into service in Adrian on June 20, 1861, at the age of eighteen as a private in Company G. He survived the war and was mustered out in Detroit on June 30, 1864, at the expiration of his enlistment.

Chapter Five
The Aftermath

We've been fighting tonight on the old camp ground
many are lying near.
Some are dead and some are dying
many are in tears.

Many are the hearts that are weary tonight
wishing for the war to cease
Many are the hearts looking for the right
to see the dawn of peace.[1]

The carnage that befell the 4th Michigan that hot, fateful Pennsylvania afternoon of July 2, 1863, was staggering indeed. Perhaps nothing bespeaks the savagery of war better than an examination of the changing fighting strength of a military unit. The 4th Michigan left Adrian in June of 1861 with a fighting strength of 1,025 officers and men. As of early September, 1862, following the Seven Days Battles, which included Mechanicsville, Gaines' Mill, White Oak Swamp and Malvern Hill, the regiment's fighting strength had declined to an astounding 288 officers and men. Between September 1862 and July 1, 1863, the unit's enrollment had grown to 342 through recruitment and draft. As the sun set on July 2, 1863, only fifty-five men were together. By morning, thirty-three more had joined the ranks and by the evening of July 3 another fifty-one men had straggled back to the regiment, bringing the total survivors of the Wheatfield to 139.[2]

Sources do not agree on the exact impact of the battle upon the fighting strength of the 4th, but all evaluations are reasonably similar. According to Colonel Sweitzer's report of July 31, 1863, the 4th entered the deadly field with 342 officers and men and came out with 139; a loss of 203 officers and men. General Barnes' report of August 24, 1863, shows a revised casualty

1. Walter Kittredge, "Tenting on the Old Campground" (N.p., 1864).
2. *OR*, vol. 27, pt. 1, p. 613.

number of 165. Detailed research yields a list of 189 casualties. By today's standards, a casualty rate in excess of ten or even fifteen percent would be considered atrocious. The 4th Michigan lost in excess of fifty-five percent of its men, yet this kind of loss was not without precedence during the Civil War.[3]

Soldiers' letters, diaries, and official correspondence can more effectively describe the battle and its aftermath. As Lieutenant Bancroft wrote, "Darkness closed the fight and we spend the night gathering the wounded." The truce, ending about dawn, occurred during a seventy-six degree, full moon-lit night with a breeze out of the south. The work must have been physically difficult and mentally draining as the rescuers listened to the moans, groans, calls for water and calls for help as they searched the field of battle.[4]

Pvt. John F. Baker was serving with Company A when he received two wounds, one in the right hip and one in the right hand. The nature of the wounds indicate that he may have been wounded during the retreat, for the bullet entered from the "posterior" and "passed upwards to the last lumbar vertebrae." During their retreat the men of the 4th had to go back up the slope of the Wheatfield; thus, the Confederates were firing upward from lower ground. Baker survived the war, discharged on October 6, 1864, at the conclusion of his term of service. Twenty-two-year-old Pvt. Isaiah Regal, also of Company A, received a gunshot wound in the left forearm that fractured the bones. It appears the wound did not require an amputation. Regal survived the war, and was discharged due to disability on June 27, 1865, from the Invalid Corps to which he had been transferred on January 1, 1864.[5]

Edward Taylor writes:

> Dear Mother:
> I take this first chance to let you know that I am safe from the battle of the day before yesterday and yesterday—the slaughter was awful but so far all is in our favor—I was taken prisoner by a party of "Rebs," and

---

3. *Ibid.*, pt.1, p. 613; *ibid.*, p. 179. A review of the *Official Records*, state regimental records, letters, and pension files permits the compilation of a casualty list chart which identifies, by company, those soldiers who were killed, wounded, missing in action or taken prisoner. The chart appears as Appendix One.
4. John Bancroft to Michigan Adjutant General, December 22, 1863, Heckert Collection.
5. Brown, *Record Fourth Michigan*, pp. 9, 92; Isaiah Regal, Pension Records, National Archives.

was sent to their rear but managed to escape when they were repulsed by playing wounded and hiding behind a large rock—I will tell my adventures another time. We took 300 men into the fight and brought out 88. I had a narrow escape. There is a lull in the storm. What comes next is hard to tell. I escaped my captors before they had time to parole me and so am good for the next fight. No more at present. When I can, I will write again.

Your affectionate son,
Edward H. C. Taylor
July 4, 1863
[Company A][6]

Lieutenant Barrett helps paint a mental picture of the battle for the Wheatfield: "It was now dusk; the fierce struggle was over for the night. The struggle had been simply terrible; the carnage was awful; the fire incessant. Groans and oaths of the wounded were heard on every hand. Many would have recovered, had they had care. But it was impossible to reach all." Barrett "was loaded into an ambulance, at two o'clock in the morning of July 3d, and taken to an old house to the north and east of the battle ground. Here were many wounded." Concerning Barrett's leg wound and his disability discharge, acting Surg. J. S. Watts wrote on November 23, 1863, "I hereby certify that I have carefully examined said Officer and find him suffering from gun shot wound received at the battle of Gettysburg Pa. In the left leg the ball entered the upper end of the middle thigh injuring both bones." Lieutenant Barrett was fortunate in two respects. First, though wounded, he survived the battle. Second, at the time of the battle he was carrying 400 dollars on his person, the money having been returned to him following the severe wounding of Chaplain Seage. He still had his life and his hard-earned pay with him at the end of the battle.[7]

Sgt. Lester H. Salsbury, twenty-three, advanced in the Wheatfield with Company B. His wounds are a further testimony to the severity of the struggle. Sergeant Salsbury received three wounds, "one ball passed through his left lung, one through his [left] arm, and one lodged in his right thigh." Salsbury's most severe wound was the one striking the left

---

6. Edward Taylor to his mother, July 4, 1863, Michigan Historical Collection.
7. Barrett, *Old Fourth Michigan*, p. 23; Brown, *Record Fourth Michigan*, p. 10; Orvey Barrett, Pension Records, National Archives.

lung; it appears that he was hit from an angle, in that the ball was "penetrating the lower lobe of the left lung... entering the chest laterally passing obliquely upwards & outwards." Sergeant Salsbury rejoined the 4th Michigan after four months of medical care, but ultimately was discharged on disability on January 23, 1864, at Bealeton, Virginia. He later became a notary public whose name appears prominently on many disability affidavits.[8]

Pvt. George Divelbess, a twenty-three-year-old member of Company B from Steuben County, Indiana, was fortunate to survive his wound. He was wounded in both thighs by a single round. It is unclear if he received his wound at the initial engagement when the Confederates emerged on three fronts or during the 4th's retreat. The "ball entered from behind just above the right (& center) gluteal fold [junction of buttocks and thigh], passing forward & inwards & emerged at the junction of the thigh & scrotum behind & again entered the lt [left] leg opposite & passed forwards & outwards & emerged in front of the femoral artery." Had the femoral artery been severed, Private Divelbess could have bled to death. George Divelbess recovered from his wounds and successfully served out his time of enlistment being mustered out as a corporal on June 30, 1864, after which he returned to his home state of Indiana. Leg wounds appear to have been commonplace for soldiers of Company B, as Alonzo Bellows, Andrew Wheaton and Larned Partridge each received wounds in the leg. Each man survived the war, and Larned Partridge would receive another wound at Spotsylvania.[9]

Twenty-eight-year-old Capt. Ebenezer French led Company C into the Wheatfield and in doing so received a gunshot wound in an arm. This was his second wound; he was wounded at Fredericksburg on December 13, 1862. Following a two and one half month recovery he returned to the regiment on March 1, 1863. Captain French was discharged on disability on May 9, 1864, but re-entered the service as captain of Company E of the re-organized 11th Infantry. Thirty-one-year-old Pvt. James C. Flera perhaps entered the battle with a need to redeem his good name. Prior to the battle of Fredericksburg, he wore the stripes of a non-commissioned officer. These chevrons, however, were taken away based on charges of cowardice. Then, in the Wheat-

8. *Hudson Gazette*, July, 1, 1888, Hudson Historical Museum, Hudson, Michigan; Brown, *Record Fourth Michigan*, p. 96; Lester H. Salsbury, Pension Records, National Archives.
9. Brown, *Record Fourth Michigan*, pp. 12, 36, 85, 120; Larned Partridge, Pension Records, National Archives.

Dearborn Historical Museum

Ebenezer French

Ebenezer French, of St. Joseph County, was twenty-six when he accepted his commission as second lieutenant of Company C on June 20, 1861. He received a commission to first lieutenant on September 1, 1861, and to captain on September 1, 1862. He was wounded at Fredericksburg in 1862 and again at Gettysburg. He was discharged on disability on May 9, 1864. He reentered the service as captain in the Reorganized 11th Michigan on March 1, 1865, and served until his discharge on September 16, 1865.

field, he redeemed his name by beating the odds. He was shot twice, one ball "passing obliquely through the right thigh opening the deep femoral artery nearly losing his life by hemmorage." Private Flera survived the war, discharged at the end of his term of enlistment on June 30, 1864, though "badly disabled." He returned to his native Indiana. Pvt. William Cooper had an extremely close call when he "received wound over right ear." He would receive a second wound on May 5, 1864. Thirty-three-year-old Pvt. Henry Beal was wounded in the upper right shoulder and was left on the field, where he was taken prisoner. He was confined at Richmond from July 21-25, 1863, and paroled on August 2 at City Point, Virginia. On August 3 he was admitted to the hospital at Annapolis, Maryland, where he remained until December 10. At that time he returned to the regiment to remain in active service until his discharge on June 30, 1864, the conclusion of his term of service. Beal then traveled north to the logging community of Manistee, Michigan, along the shores of Lake Michigan where he lived until his death in November 1894.[10]

Pvt. Epaminondas Thurston, twenty-three, of Company C, survived his wound after two months of hospitalization at Summit House Hospital in Philadelphia. He returned to the regiment and was wounded and taken prisoner at Fredericksburg on May 6, 1864. He was transferred to Andersonville Prison on May 31, 1864, and survived the unspeakable conditions of prison life to be paroled at Jacksonville, Florida, on April 28, 1865. Twenty-five-year-old Sgt. Don Rickett was shot in the back of the left shoulder with the ball exiting from his chest, possibly injuring the upper portion of his left lung. Sergeant Rickett's wound would be consistent with either the early part of the engagement or during the retreat. Rickett was also shot in the upper right thigh. He was hospitalized at Summit House Hospital where he recovered and returned to the regiment to serve the balance of his term of enlistment. He was mustered out on June 29, 1864.[11]

Disability records for Pvt. Jacob Bensler of Company D reveal that the 4th had to contend with artillery as well as musket fire. Private Bensler "incurred an injury to his right shoulder by being struck by a piece of shell while in action.... Our position at the time being partly in the woods and Wheatfield near Little Round Top Mountain." This suggests

10. *Ibid.*, pp. 11, 29, 42, 44; Henry Beal, Pension Records, National Archives.
11. Brown, *Record Fourth Michigan*, pp. 93, 110; Don Rickett, Pension Records, National Archives.

that Bensler was in Trostle's Woods preparing to re-enter the Wheatfield. Bensler continued to serve until his discharge for disability on August 22, 1865, from the re-organized 4th Michigan.[12]

The disability papers for forty-two-year-old Pvt. John J. Dates of Company D provide insight of how quick the men of the 4th were moving as they exited the Wheatfield. Private Dates received a "severe gunshot wound left thigh." Testimony continues "that [as the] Reg't was retreating, he stumbled & fell, at the time he recovered his feet he was wounded as alleged, that his Co. was some 10 rods [over 50 yards] ahead of him." Private Dates was recovered by Union troops then "taken to Field Hosp. thence to York, Pa." Dates did not recover sufficiently to return to duty. He was discharged for disability on January 19, 1864.[13]

Pvt. James Hudler, thirty-one, of Company D, was so severely wounded that he lost a limb. Private Hudler was shot in the left leg, fracturing the bones and resulted in amputation above the knee. He received a discharge for disability on May 27, 1864. Pvt. William Cronenwill was admitted to the general hospital at York, Pennsylvania, on July 20 with two wounds; one in his right thigh and one in his right leg. Although he recovered from his wounds, he was unable to maintain the pace and rigors of an army on campaign and was thus transferred to the Invalid Corps on January 15, 1864.[14]

Pvt. Anton Bauer, twenty-nine, of Company D also received multiple wounds in the melee. Private Bauer received a wound in "the left arm fracturing the bone near the shoulder" and "in the left side." Fortunately, he did not lose his arm. On February 15, 1864, he was transferred to the Invalid Corps.[15]

A letter written by Quimby Hugh Crawford of Company D from a Gettysburg hospital and printed in a Monroe, Michigan, newspaper describes Crawford's head wound and wound over an eye. The letter also notes that the company went into the fight with thirty-four men and came out with only five. Barrett recorded the suffering of an unidentified member of Company D: "One poor fellow of our regiment, a Company D man, was

---

12. *Record Fourth Michigan*, p. 13; Jacob Bensler, Pension Records, National Archives.
13. Brown, *Record Fourth Michigan*, p. 33; John J. Dates, Pension Records, National Archives.
14. Brown, *Record Fourth Michigan*, pp. 31, 58; James Hudler, Pension Records, National Archives.
15. Brown, *Record Fourth Michigan*, p. 11; Anton Butler, Pension Records, National Archives.

shot in the head. He would get on his knees, put his head on the ground, and twist his head in the ground. He bored that way until death put an end to his sufferings."[16]

Cpl. Edward M. Taylor of Company E received his wound as the Confederates came off Stony Hill. Disability records attest to the trajectory of the ball. Corporal Taylor was wounded in the left leg when the "ball entered posteriorly at middle of upper third of leg and traversed the whole length of leg and was extracted 3 1/2 mo's afterwards just behind the ancle [ankle]." Taylor was shot from behind by someone at a higher elevation. The only time the Confederates held higher ground is when they came down Stony Hill into the Wheatfield upon the right flank and rear of the 4th. Taylor did not fully recover from his wound. He was discharged on disability on February 24, 1864.[17]

The *Hudson Gazette* reported: "We have only ten men left in our Company and not much over one hundred in the regiment. Hiram Fountain and Addison of our company [F] were killed and afterwards found and buried by us. [Second] Lieutenant [Benjamin E.] Westfall and his brother [Pvt. Charles Westfall] were slightly wounded." Lieutenant Westfall led Company F into the battle and was "some feet in advance of his company at the time he received the wound" in his right hand. His company entered the fray with twenty-six men but came out of the Wheatfield with only six, leaving twenty comrades behind either killed, wounded or captured—a casualty rate of seventy-seven percent. Westfall was among the wounded; he "was severely wounded in his right hand; one ball grazed his neck enough to make a scar; one ball shot his haversack straps in two; and one other perforated a rain coat he carried on his left arm." His brother, Pvt. Charles Westfall, also of Company F, received more serious wounds, having been struck twice: once in the right arm and in the right elbow. He was hospitalized in Germantown, Pennsylvania. The Westfall brothers had migrated from New York to Michigan in 1860 with their parents and eleven siblings. Following the war, Benjamin Westfall became a carpenter and a justice of the peace and lived until 1924.[18]

In a letter dated July 5, 1863, William H. Tolford of Company F wrote:

---

16. *Monroe Commerical*, September 3, 1863; Barrett, *Old Fourth Michigan*, p. 24.
17. Brown, *Record Fourth Michigan*, p. 108; Edward M. Taylor, Pension Records, National Archives.
18. *Hudson Gazette*, July 11, 1863; *ibid.*, May 3, 1924.

Dear Family and Friends:

I am happy to inform you that I am safe; but I have sad news to tell you concerning the rest of the Company and regiment. We arrived on Thursday last soon after the fight commenced and immediately ordered to the front. In the afternoon we were ordered to support a battery. The battery soon became disabled, and we were ordered to charge on the rebels. We did so and in doing it were flanked on two sides by the rebels which exposed us to a severe cross fire. We were nearly surrounded before we were ordered to retreat. Col. Jeffords was wounded on the way back and afterwards died. Our loss in killed, wounded and missing is very great. We have only ten men left in our company and not much over one hundred in the regiment. Hiram Fountain and Addison, of our Company, were killed, and afterwards found and buried by us. Lieut. Westfall and his brother were slightly wounded. We have since learned that six of our men were prisoners, and unhurt. Noah Webster and myself are all that remain of the boys from Pittsford. Albert Boise was taken prisoner, and escaped in the night. He says that Irwin Miner and Beal Dillion with four others are prisoners.

We have taken a great number of prisoners and according to all accounts have got the rebel army to a pretty tight place. We had no fighting near us yesterday, and but little the day before. We heard some cannonading to the left of us, in the rear of the enemy, and it was supposed by some that the rebels were trying to escape. Others thought that reinforcements were coming to us, and in the rear of the enemy.

I could not tell all the news concerning our march from Virginia, and the fight here, if I were to write all day. Suffice it to say, we had a very rough time of it; but we are thankful that we are no worse off. Our regiment may not be called to go into the fight again, very soon, on account of our colonel. I hope to hear from you soon. I remain as ever your affectionate friend and husband.

W. M. H. Tolford[19]

---

19. W. M. H. Tolford to family and friends, July 5, 1863, Hudson Historical Museum; *Hudson Gazette*, July 7, 1863, Hudson Historical Museum; Brown, *Record Fourth Michigan*, p. 110.

Monroe County Historical Commission

Benjamin Westfall

Benjamin Westfall, of Hudson, Michigan, was twenty-two when he entered the service at Adrian on June 20, 1861, as corporal in Company F. He held the rank of first sergeant and was second lieutenant of Company F as of March 7, 1863, at the time of the Wheatfield battle. Westfall was wounded at Gettysburg. He was in command of Company F from August, 1863 through April, 1864 and received a second wound on June 19, 1864. He was mustered out at the expiration of his service on June 29, 1864, in Detroit.

Sometime after May 5, 1864, the "family and friends" of William Henry Tolford received the dreaded news of his death in the Wilderness battle.

According to pension records, Moses Morgan of Company G was wounded in the battle. He received "a wound in the left leg just above the ankle caused by a minnie-rifle ball . . . he was engaged with his regiment and his company in the battle of Gettysburg, as we were falling back from the line of battle ... and lay on the battlefield until about 2 the next morning." Morgan recovered and returned to the regiment. He received a second wound while at Petersburg in August, 1864 that resulted in his disability discharge on February 9, 1866.[20]

Lieutenant Bancroft noted, "of the 23 men in Company H five were killed, [Charles W.] Gregery, [George] Purdy, [James H.] Pendleton, [Joseph] Brink, [Charles H.] Wilson. Captain [William F.] Robinson was wounded and a prisoner and Lieutenant [Samuel G.] Walker was wounded. Lieutenant [Michael] Vreeland was severely wounded." Captain Robinson, twenty-six, of Company H wrote on December 22, 1863, of men and materiel losses: "The regiment to which my company belongs was directed to advance under the fire of the enemy to take a certain position in so doing 4 privates and 1 non-commissioned officer were killed; 7 privates and 1 non-commissioned officer severely wounded, and 3 privates and 1 non-commissioned officer taken prisoners. . . . The arms carried by all these men were left on the field, as we were repulsed, and they could not be recovered." Total casualties of Company H were seventeen out of twenty-three. Further testimony of the fierceness of the fight was recorded by Robinson following the July 2 engagement on Form No. 9, "Materials Expended or Consumed," as found in the State of Michigan papers: "1,482 elongated ball cartridges and 1,642 percussion caps," or an average of sixty-four rounds per soldier.[21]

Robinson also penned a letter to his father from his hospital bed in Marietta, Pennsylvania, on July 22, 1863:

Dear Father:
I rec'd your kind letter of the 15th inst. this noon, and as I wrote you yesterday that I had not heard from

20. Brown, *Record Fourth Michigan*, p. 110; *ibid.*, p. 79; Moses Morgan, Pension Records, National Archives.
21. John Bancroft to Michigan Adjutant General, December 22, 1863, Michigan Historical Collection; Affadavit sworn to George L. Maltz, acting adjutant, December 22, 1863, Michigan Historical Collection; Form No. 9, State of Michigan Papers, Michigan Historical Collection.

any of you, I thought it my duty to acknowledge the receipt of it immediately. As I wrote you it is nothing but a flesh wound and I shall be able to walk with crutches in a little over a week. I sat up to have it dressed this morning for the first time. There is no need of Mothers coming down here, but I thought that if you had time that it would be a pleasant trip for you, and that you could assist me about obtaining a leave. I should be very happy to see Mother, but as far as nursing is concerned I have the best. I used nothing but cold water, I was washed all over the first week twice a day, now every morning. My wound is doing beautifully, it has nearly stopped supperating and has begun to granulate.

Good bye, Love to all
William

P.S. I will write more when I can sit up.
WELL[22]

Lt. Michael Vreeland of Company I, severely wounded and narrowly escaping death by bayonet, lay on the battlefield. He later recalled in a letter: "My last recollection of the day was the blood red sun sinking in the west through the smoke and haze of the battle. A sun I never expected to see again."[23] Vreeland attested to the equipment lost in the Wheatfield:

> I certify on honor that on 2nd day of July 1863 at Gettysburg Pa. the stores enumerated below were lost under the following circumstance. The right wing of the regiment to which my company belonged was surrounded by the enemy; of my company five killed, ten wounded, and the remainder taken prisoners [7]. The arms and accoutrements carried by these men were left on the field and not recovered.[24]

The entire force of twenty-two men were casualties. Vreeland was charged with the cost of the lost equipment, approximately

---

22. William F. Robinson to his father, July 22, 1863, Michigan Historical Collection.
23. Michael Vreeland to Mary Vreeland, date unknown, Vreeland family papers, Cecile Vreeland Collection, Waldport, Oregon.
24. *Ibid.*

$370. He tried until his death in 1876 to recover the cost from the U.S. government but failed.[25]

Pension records for Second Lt. R. Watson Seage of Company I describe his multiple wounds and attest to the fierceness of the battle: "a gunshot wound through the right lung, the ball passing in through the muscles and nerves of the right arm losing the use of the right arm; and a gunshot wound through the left breast; also two bayonet wounds in the left leg above the knee." Henry S. Seage adds further insight in his post-war letter: "After our regiment had taken up a new position, I was permitted to go over the field in search of my brother's body, which I found about daylight the following morning, insensible but still alive. We carried him back to a field hospital, of what corps I can't now tell." Lieutenant Seage did not sufficiently recover from his wounds to permit him to rejoin the 4th. He was discharged for disability on December 31, 1863. Dedicated to the Cause as he was, he re-entered the service on August 2, 1864, as regimental quartermaster for the Reorganized 4th Michigan. His Gettysburg wounds, however, continued to plague him, resulting in a second disability discharge on March 6, 1865. One week later he received the rank of brevet captain of U.S. Volunteers.[26]

James Houghton of Company K recorded the death of his tent mate, James Johnson, who was killed in the Wheatfield near Rose's Woods while the regiment was beginning their retreat. "He was but a few feet in front of me when he fell. I heard him say 'I am killed' this was the last words that I heard

---

25. His wife continued the effort until 1900. Strange, that an officer of the army would be charged with the cost of equipment lost in a battle. Army regulations, however, did hold officers responsible. Article #40 of the Articles of War states, "Every captain of a troop or company is charged with the arms, accoutrements, ammunition, clothing, or other warlike stores belonging to the troop or company under his command." Rule #1332 of the Pay Department supports Article #40. Rule #1332 reads, "Authorized stoppages to reimburse the United States, as for loss or damage to arms, equipment." Rules #1339, #1421 and #1425 of the Ordnance Department all address the responsibility of filing ordnance and property returns and specify that such returns are to be filed "within twenty days after the quarter." Lieutenant Vreeland's trouble began when he failed to file Form 1, Quarterly Return of Ordnance Stores Received, Issued and Remaining On Hand. He failed to file Form 1 because of his wounds and subsequent hospitalization. He later issued the letter that appeared earlier in this paragraph in an effort to comply with the subject rules and regulations. His efforts to rectify the situation and to recover the lost wages were unsuccessful.
26. Henry Seage to John Bachelder, September 23, 1884 in Ladd, The Bachelder Papers, pp. 1070-73; Brown, *Record Fourth Michigan*, p. 98; Richard Watson Seage, Pension Records, National Archives.

him speak the rest was groans there was no help for him." Johnson was a nineteen-year-old draftee from Shiawassee Township who was mustered into nine month service on February 20, 1863.[27] On July 4 Houghton continued his narrative:

> Wishing to know that my tent mate decently buried, I procured a pass for myself and a fellow by the name of George Tracey [Company K]. We started out going over a portion of the ground where Picke[t]ts great charge terminated. In many places it was inconvenient to walk without stepping in clods of human blood. It was Rebel blood so it did not seem so bad.... When we arrived at the wheatfield we found men there busily engaged in burying the dead. They informed me that they had just got my tent mate buried. They showed me his grave. His knapsack and haversack still lying on the ground where he fell. He had recently bought a new tin cup which was buckled onto his haversack. I took hold of it thinking I would take it for a keepsake. Examining it a little closer found that a large minnie ball had passed through his haversack and went into his person. I was told by the men that buried him that there were seven ball holes in his person.[28]

As previously noted, Capt. James B. McLean of Company K was wounded during the battle and helped from the field. Captain McLean received his wound as he neared the relative safety of the Pennsylvania Reserves who the 4th passed through as they exited the Wheatfield.[29] Private Houghton recorded how he helped his captain off the field:

> Our Captain James B. McLean was wounded in the chin, left leg & heel but could yet hobble along. He asked me to aid him in getting to the hospital. I told him that I would do what I could for him. I carried all of his things even to his sword and belt. He said his sword hurt the wound on his leg. He put his hand on my shoulder and hobbled along. We took an old road that went winding through the woods between the two Round Tops. This was the road that the principle part of the

---

27. Brown, *Record Fourth Michigan*, p. 61.
28. Houghton journal, July 4, 1863.
29. James B. McLean, Pension Records, National Archives.

wounded had been passing during the day. It was a very frequent occurrence to see pools of blood along the road where the poor fellows had stopped a few moments to rest. Some were sitting under trees by the road side apparently too weak to go any further. There was not ambulance wagons enough to carry only the worst cases. Captain McLean was so weakened from loss of blood that he frequently had to stop and rest. Blood was gushing in his boots every step he took and blood was also running down his long chin whiskers from the wound on his chin causing a fearful appearance. After going about a half a mile east of little Round Top we came to a 3d Corps hospital. This hospital was situated in a barn yard. As we came to the gate we were met by a guard who informed us that they had about 300 wounded in the hospital and could not possibly admit any more. The captain was too weak to go any farther so he laid down on the ground saying he would lie there till they could take him in. I passed through the gate where the wounded were lying and a fearful sight met my gaze. The wounded were lying on the ground in rows across the yard with aisles between for the waiters and surgeons to pass through. At the east end of the yard were lying some of the most hopeless cases. Some were wreathing in agonies of death waiting only for the messenger of death to claim its victim. I took one of the aisles that led to the west end of the yard. Here the surgeons were busily at work probing for bullets and amputating limbs. It requires a man with steel nerves and a case hardened heart to be a Army Surgeon. At this moment the battle was raging more fierce than ever. At the Round Tops clouds of smoke were rolling up as [if] a dozen steam engines were there at work. The boom of cannons, the crash of musketry was incessant. The war clouds were rolling up in it's wildest form which actually shaded the hospital and added gloom to the occasion. From where the surgeons were at work I took an aisle which led into the barn. The barn was filled with the wounded to its utmost capacity and if I ever hear a barn full of groans it was there. It was more than I could stand. I soon made my way back to the gate where the captain was lying. He gave me his sword and belt and requested me to give it to our first lieutenant. So I started out in search of our regiment. I had not

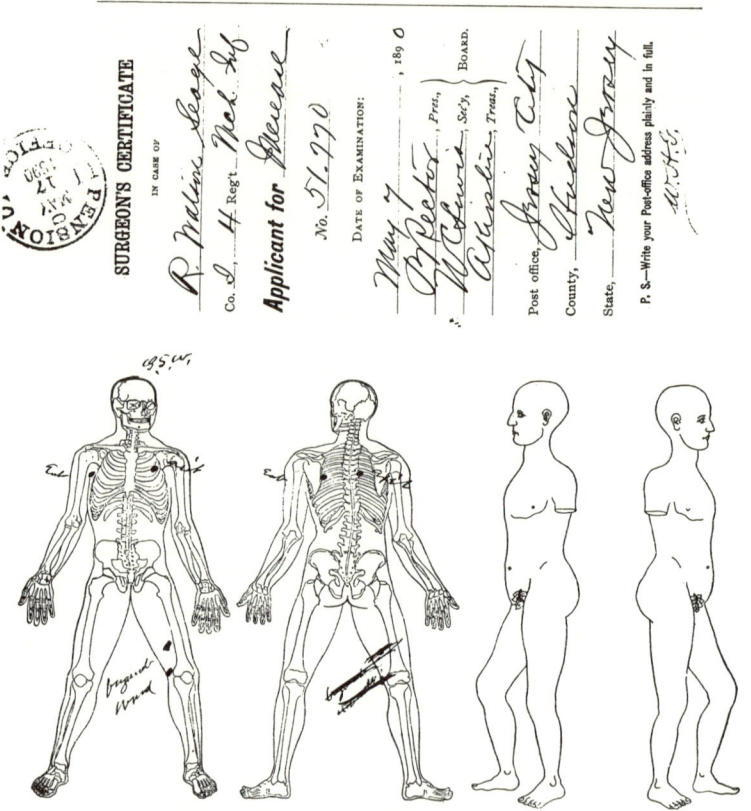

National Archives

Surgeon Certificate of Richard Watson Seage

When Civil War veterans who had suffered an injury during their period of service applied for a disability pension it was required that they have a Surgeon's Certificate attesting to the nature of the injury, when it was received, how it was received and an estimation of its severity. Surgeon Certificates typically included diagrams of a man upon which the attending physician would mark the location of the injury. This Surgeon's Certificate was for Richard Watson Seage. It clearly shows two gun shot wounds ("G.S.W.") that passed through his chest at an angle. It also shows two bayonet wounds on the left thigh just above the knee. All wounds were received at the Wheatfield. This Surgeon's Certificate is dated May 7, 1890.

gone far when I met the Lieutenant coming. I gave him the sword and told him of the captain's condition. He replied we must get him away from there so we went back to where the captain was lying. The Lieutenant borrowed a stretcher. We got the captain on it and carried him to another hospital. Here his wounds were dressed and he was well cared for. As soon as possible I returned to little Round Top in search of my regiment. It was now quite dusk out. I soon made my way to the east side of little Round Top where we first started from but my regiment was not there. I was tired out and sat down on a log to rest and in spite of my hardest efforts to keep awake, I fell asleep and knew no more till I awoke in the morning when I found myself well incumbered with leaves and rubish by the side of the log.[30]

What Houghton does not record is that Captain McLean had contracted tuberculosis of the left lung in the "winter of 62 & 1863." Consequently, his breathing capacity was impaired, particularly when under pressure and tension. Houghton also commented on the size of companies after the battle; "before leaving Gettysburg Company K, I, and C were consolidated into one company and the 3 Companys numbered only 34 men."[31]

General Barnes paid tribute to Colonel Jeffords' dedication to duty and personal sacrifice in his report dated August 24, 1863: "A special mention should also be made of Colonel Jeffords, of the Fourth Michigan Volunteers, who sealed his devotion to his country with his blood, while contending hand to hand with overpowering numbers, in endeavoring to rescue the colors of his regiment from the hands of the enemy."[32]

These soldiers' words speak volumes about their historic struggle, yet they leave a great deal unsaid about the savagery of the battle. A trait quite common of their time. With casualties as extensive as the 4th Michigan's one would think the unit would have been placed on inactive service pending consolidation with other Michigan infantry regiments; but not so. Throughout the day of July 3, the remnants of the 4th regrouped and prepared to participate in the pursuit.

---

30. Houghton journal, July 4, 1863.
31. James B. McLean, Pension Records, National Archives; Houghton journal, July 4, 1863.
32. *OR*, vol. 27, pt.1, p. 604.

Chapter Six
The Pursuit

The 4th Michigan withdrew from the Wheatfield in small groups. For the balance of the night and on July 3, the survivors regrouped. As Lieutenant Bancroft recorded, the regiment "lay in position behind a stone wall on Little Round Top." The position Bancroft refers to is an area behind the Weikert farmhouse. The Weikert farm, located behind the woods bearing the family name, had been turned into a field hospital. It most certainly must have been a horrific sight to behold with wounded laying all around; the most severely wounded were set further away so that those who might be saved could be aided by the over-worked, under-staffed medical corps. Despite their dwindling numbers, the 4th Michigan was held in reserve, ready to move to any quarter to support their brothers. They would, however, see no further action at Gettysburg. From their reserve position, in sweltering eighty-seven degree heat, they would only listen to Longstreet's Charge.[1]

The survivors of the Wheatfield spent much time searching for lost comrades, going to hospitals and to neighboring units. Corporal Seage recalled that he:

> started with a stretcher with some of the pioneer corps and went to the front to a hospital to get Col. Jeffords. Soon found him and brought him down to our regimental hospital. He died yesterday from wounds one ball through the leg, a bayonet wound through the side. The pioneers carried him back and will try to send him home. Moved then down to the Division hospital. I put up tent and eat dinner, while doing so some of the boys came in and told me Dick [R. Watson Seage] had come. Went out and saw him on a stretcher. The doctor dressed his wound and took a ball out of his left side.

---

1. Gregory Coco, *A Vast Sea of Misery* (Gettysburg: Thomas, 1988), pp. 68-70; Jacobs, "Meteorology of the Battle," pp. 120-21. The 4th was encamped opposite the Leister house.

Soon after moved all the wounded to the corps hospital. Battle continued.[2]

A major change in leadership also took place, one that appears to have pleased the troops—General Griffin returned and relieved General Barnes.

By 2 p.m. on July 4, the temperature dropped back to a tolerable seventy-two degrees and rains commenced to wash the battlefields of blood. The Confederates had begun their retreat back to Virginia and members of the 4th Michigan went back to the field of battle to search for comrades, locate discarded equipment and bury their dead. Henry Seage recorded that "brigade trains came up with wall tents, put them up and moved the wounded into them." He continued that he attempted to forage for additional food, but found little in the immediate area: "went out in country with horse, go get supplies, could only get onions."[3]

On July 5 the Fifth Corps was on the march in a southerly direction leaving Gettysburg by 5 p.m. The Fifth and Eleventh Corps, under General Howard, were ordered to Middletown via Emmitsburg, Creagerstown, Utica and High Knob Pass. On July 1 the regiment would have extended about one-half mile along the road; on July 5 it covered a mere one eighth of a mile. The Fifth Corps marched approximately five miles, pulled off the road and massed in the field to await further orders from General Howard. Seage stayed behind in Gettysburg and found time to write four letters: two for Lieutenant Vreeland who had been badly wounded on July 2, one to his brother and one home. He also recorded that the chaplain brought supplies, including brandy. The day ended at 9:30 p.m. near Emmitsburg along the south side of Marsh Creek with more rain.[4]

Shortly after 10 a.m. on July 6, the 4th Michigan was moved a short distance to re-establish its camp "near Moritz farm, where the Fairfield road joins the Emmitsburg and Gettysburg road." Lieutenant Bancroft noted that "The Army is passing [First and Third Corps]. Roads are very muddy and soft" and that they "march in the fields." It was apparently an uneventful day, as Corporal Seage "went over to 2nd Corps hospital for Vreeland."[5] Corporal Taylor penned a short letter to his sister:

2. Seage journal, July 3, 1863.
3. Jacobs, "Meterology of the Battle," pp. 120-21; Seage journal, July 4, 1863.
4. *OR*, vol. 27, pt. 3, p. 530, 532, 540.
5. *Ibid.*, p. 557; Bancroft journal, July 6, 1863; Seage journal, July 6, 1863.

                              Camp 4th Mich. Infantry
                              Near Emmetsburg, Pa. [Md.]
July 6th, 1863
My dear sister
   I write a few lines to let you know that I have come through the late battle "all right". I will give all particulars when I can write at liesure. Till then good by— Write soon.
                              Affectionately Your Brother
                                   Edw. H. C. Taylor
                              Address 4th Mich. Infty.
                                 1st Division, 5th Corps
                                   Army of Potomac[6]

Also on that day, General Warren wrote a dispatch to Gen. William F. Smith on behalf of General Meade, to bring his troops up from Gettysburg as they were no longer needed there. In this dispatch Warren recorded the sentiment of the Union concerning the Gettysburg engagement: "We have made this place a sore subject of mention to Southern pride."[7]

The march south, back through Maryland, continued on July 7 with the Fifth Corps rising at 4 a.m. and breaking camp at 6 a.m. marching twenty miles to within six miles of Frederick by 6 p.m. near High Knob behind the Eleventh Corps. The rain continued in the evening. The 4th was up early on the 8th and marched ten miles in the rain to Middletown, Maryland. By noon the skies had cleared, records Bancroft. Of special interest was the dispatch received by General Howard that reads, in part: "Leave your men whose shoes are worn out, and send them for shoes."[8] It is unclear if anyone from the 4th stayed behind to get new shoes. Bancroft recounted that, having arrived by 4 p.m. and encamped at Middletown, "Davis took the horse & went to Middletown for turnips."[9]

The pursuit of the Army of Northern Virginia continued at 5 a.m. on July 9, a clear day, with a six mile march over South Mountain via Fox Gap to Boonsborough, Maryland. General Sykes established Fifth Corps headquarters "between

---

6. Edward Taylor to his sister, July 6, 1863, Michigan Historical Collection.
7. *Ibid.*, pp. 557, 560, 579.
8. *OR*, vol. 27, pt. 3, pp. 562, 586, 587; *ibid.*, pt. 1, p. 146; *ibid.*, pt. 3, p. 587.
9. Bancroft journal, July 7, 1863. It is unclear who the man referred to by Bancroft is, since there were four men in the 4th by the name of Davis during the Gettysburg campaign. It is certain, however, that it was not James Davis of Company I, since he was taken prisoner in the Wheatfield and not returned to the regiment until October 9, 1863.

Rohrersville and Boonsborough," at the intersection of the Sharpsburg, Rohrersville and Boonsborough Roads, where he awaited the Third Corps to close upon the Fifth Corps. There the regiment encamped at 9 a.m. Henry Seage, having stayed in Gettysburg, recorded that he observed "several citizens came in to hospital with provisions." Seage went on that he visited his brother and "put up Dick's poncho for him outside [the] big tent." Dick apparently could not "stay in the big tent on account of noises."[10]

On July 10 the regiment was ordered to the bridge over Antietam Creek above Sharpsburg near Roxbury Mills, a distance of eight miles. By 3 p.m. the First Division had reached Jones' Crossroads, according to a report issued by Col. James C. Rice of the Third Brigade. Bancroft recorded hearing firing in the front. While it was an uneventful day for the regiment as a whole, it was a very special day indeed for Henry Seage and his wounded brother: "Nothing of importance during the day until about 5pm. We were surprized and astonished at the arrival of brother Ed. He stayed with us and took up a soldier bed for the first time. His bed consisted of our rubber poncho over and under us. Tonight is the first time us three brothers have slept side by side for 3 years. Slept first rate."[11]

The men of the 4th had marched fifty-five miles since leaving Gettysburg on July 5, or an average of nine miles per day. The regiment continued the southern march on July 11 by moving "up the Antietam." Bancroft recounted that they "form line, 'close in mass,' move forward about six p.m., leveling fences, etc, wheat and corn. Infantry, artillery and ambulances."[12] It was a "grand sight" he recalled, probably refering to Maj. Gen. Andrew A. Humphreys's order of 3 p.m.:

> Advance your line of battle to near the position now occupied by your skirmishers, and make your skirmish line connect with General Sedgewick's, on the Antietam Creek. Then push forward to reconnoiter between the creek and Sharpsburg pike, and drive the enemy toward Funkstown, till he is found superior in force. It is not the intention that you should support this force further than to assist its return, if pressed. The Third Corps will be moved up to the rear of your line. Similar

10. *OR*, vol. 27, pt. 3, p. 601; *ibid.*, pt.1, p. 146; *ibid.*, pt. 3, pp. 615, 616, 618; Seage journal, July 9, 1863.
11. *OR*, vol. 27, pt. 3, p. 616; *ibid.*, pt. 1, p. 621; Seage journal, July 10, 1863.
12. Bancroft journal, July 11, 1863.

reconnaissances will be made by the Sixth Corps on the opposite side of the Antietam, and by the Second Corps on the Sharpsburg pike."[13]

July 11 also marked the journey home for R. Watson Seage as brother Henry recounted. "Started at 8 o'clock AM for Gettysburg [from the field hospital]. Dick rode in a buggy. Was to late for the 10am train so had to wait for the 5pm train. Rode all night, arrived at Baltimore at 3am." Henry continued that when they arrived, "the wounded were laid on stretchers along the side walks. The relief associations dressed & fed the wounded then the Mich. officers went to the church home & infirmary on Broadway. Carried Dick on stretcher. His is a fine institution cared for in a fine style and $4.00 per week charges. This was formerly a Marine hospital."[14]

While the Seage brothers were together in Baltimore, the balance of the 4th Michigan was in Antietam Creek, Maryland. The regiment took the field and "advance as reserve to skirmishers. The 6th Corps came into position on our right in sight of the Rebel pickets making breastworks of rails and wheat." The Fifth Corps was "relieved in the afternoon" and went "to the left into the woods."[15]

July 13 the Fifth Corps marched toward Berlin in the rain. There the troops were issued new clothes according to a report issued by Colonel Lumbard to Governor Blair of Michigan in December, 1863. This report also noted that the "enemy crossed the Potomac under the cover of night." Fatigue duty was the order of the day for the 4th as remembered by Lieutenant Bancroft: "Up at daybreak. Move left of the 5th Mass. battery and make breastworks. Gen. Griffin inspects the line and we make a new line."[16]

On July 14 the regiment advanced four miles toward Williamsport in the late morning under cloudy skies. By 2 p.m., Griffin's Second Brigade was "within 2 miles of Williamsport, on the right of the Williamsport and Boonsborough road" reported General Sykes.[17] They did not encounter the Confederates as they had already crossed the Potomac into Virginia. With the Confederates went all the Union prisoners of war from Gettysburg, including those from the 4th Michigan.

13. *OR*, vol. 27, pt. 3, p. 648.
14. Seage journal, July 11, 1863; *ibid.*, July 12, 1863.
15. *Ibid.*, July 11, 1863.
16. Bancroft journal, July 13, 1863; *OR*, vol. 27, pt. 3, p. 680; Brown, *Record Fourth Michigan*, pp. 10-11. Berlin is known today as Brunswick.
17. *OR*, vol. 27, pt. 3, pp. 689-90.

By 3 a.m. on the morning of July 15, the regiment was once again on the march, in pursuit of the retreating Confederates in accordance with general orders issued on July 14 to march to Keedysville, through Fox's Gap to Burkettsville, Berlin being the objective. John Bancroft wrote that it was a "very hot" day and a "tedious" march of twenty-two miles ending "at or near Burkettsville" by 5 p.m. Bancroft's observation is supported by General Sykes' 5 p.m. dispatch to General Humphreys which reads, in part, "My men are exhausted. Several officers are reported sunstruck." Bancroft was fortunate this day as he had "a good supper at a farmhouse." Of special interest is his comment about the organization of the 4th Michigan following the Gettysburg campaign: "organize in five companies after the battle of Gettysburg."[18]

July 15 was a pivotal day for the citizens of Dexter, Michigan, as the body of their local hero came home. Col. Harrison Jeffords' funeral, held at the family residence on July 16, was reportedly attended by 2,000 people, an outstanding attendance from a small, rural community. Of further interest was that three towns expressed a desire to have the remains buried in their communities: Dexter, Lima and Ann Arbor. This demonstrated the esteem Colonel Jeffords was held by the residents of these three communities.[19]

The regiment rose early once again at 2 a.m. on the 16th and began their 4 a.m. march towards Berlin, encamping there by noon. Bancroft wrote a very difficult letter home to the loved ones of a fallen soldier. On this day he wrote a letter to Abe Purdy whose son, George, was killed in the Wheatfield. George was eighteen when he enlisted in Company H on February 11, 1863, for a period of nine months as a substitute for his father. What a shock this letter must have been; to know that your son, who took your place in the ranks, had been killed.[20] Purdy wrote a response from Marathon, Michigan, which reads, in part:

> Mr. Bancroft
> Yours of the 16th brings painful tidings for my heart, a great loss to me and my family. But when I consider the cause in which my son was engaged I forbear to grieve and hope a speedy success to all.[21]

---

18. *Ibid.*, pp. 689, 690, 695, 702.
19. *Hudson Gazette*, July 19, 1863; *Dexter Leader*, August 18, 1932.
20. Brown, *Record Fourth Michigan*, p. 90; *OR*, vol. 27, pt. 3, p. 702.
21. Bancroft journal, undated entry, 1863.

The march south continued on July 17 by 3 p.m. toward Warrenton. The 4th encamped at Lovettsville, Virginia.[22]

The pursuit continued on the 18th and 19th. Commencing at 6 a.m. on July 18 the First Division marched seven miles towards Purcellville, encamping by noon. The march resumed by 8 a.m. the following morning and ended four miles later near Purcellville where Lieutenant Bancroft once again enjoyed the hospitality of a local farmer, this time a Virginia Quaker. Bancroft recalled this day to be "very hot." On July 20 the Fifth Corps marched twelve miles south along the Rectortown road through the village of Union and encamped at the intersection of the Aldie and Ashby Gap roads. Lieutenant Bancroft recorded that he did "not feel very well" and by the 20th he was "quite sick" and riding in an ambulance all day towards Ashby Gap. The cause or nature of his illness was not recorded. Bancroft stayed in camp on the 21st and in a letter to a Mr. T. H. Hinchman he revealed the strength of the 4th Michigan as being 101 men. In the same letter he indicated that Capt. William Loveland of Company B, Capt. George Montieth of Company E and Lt. Edwin Gilbert of Company D, "are going home to get conscripts."[23]

The 4th Michigan marched through Rectortown, Virginia, on the 22nd of July en route to Piedmont, being assigned as Third Corps support. The Army of the Potomac had entered territory where straggling could be hazardous for a soldier on the march. Capt. J. C. Paine of the Signal Corps passed through Piedmont en route to Manassas Gap and included the following in his dispatch to Capt. Lemuel B. Norton, Chief Signal Officer. "This region is infested by Mosby's men; they followed me some four miles this morning."[24]

The Fifth Corps rose at 4 a.m. on July 23 and marched fifteen miles through Markham Station and Linden to Manassas Gap in support of the Third Corps, which was ordered, "if practical, [to] attack the enemy." The 4th bivouacked in the vicinity of Manassas Gap "in line of battle." The First Division, along with the Second and Third Divisions, made a reconnaissance in force "moving in line of battle near the railroad in the Gap." The Fifth Corps, having not made Confederate contact, marched back two miles and established camp. Orders to move were received on the 25th. The Fifth Corps, the last corps to leave Manassas Gap, was ordered to Warrenton "by way of

---

22. Bancroft journal, July 17, 1863; OR, vol. 27, pt. 3, p. 621.
23. Bancroft journal, July 19, 1863; *ibid.*, July 20, 1863; *OR*, vol. 27, pt. 3, pp. 718, 721, 726.
24. *Ibid*, pt. 1, p. 149; *ibid.*, pt. 3, pp. 739, 744.

Barbee's Cross-Roads." Their objective was "the Waterloo road, in front of Warrenton."[25] The Fifth Corps continued the march south at 11 a.m. on July 26, with orders to proceed through Warrenton and take up a position on the right of the Second Corps, near the Warrenton Branch Railroad and the Orange-Alexandria Railroad. The Fifth Corps deployed one division towards Fayetteville and one at Bealeton Station and remained in this deployment until July 31, when General Sykes received orders to mass his troops "in the vicinity of Fayetteville." Before July 31, the Fifth Corps moved to Beverly Ford on the Rappahannock River and there the regiment stayed until September 16.[26]

While at Beverly Ford, Lt. Col. Jarius Hall wrote the editor of the *Michigan Argus*:

> I am very glad to hear that the remains of Col. Jeffords reached their destination. It was with great difficulty that I succeeded in finding a citizen [of Gettysburg] who would take charge of the remains, and then I had many fears that he would fail. Col. Jeffords was the pride of the 4th Regiment; the command will long mourn the loss of the noble leader.[27]

The 4th Michigan had marched an encircling route in excess of 350 miles in just 60 days, and had participated in the nation's most memorable battle. In doing so they had etched their honorable name in history, forever.

---

25. *Ibid.*, p. 746; *ibid.*, pt.1, p. 149; *ibid.*, pt. 3, pp. 636, 759.
26. *Ibid.*, pp. 767, 789, 793; Brown, *Record Fourth Michigan*, p. 11.
27. *Michigan Argus* [Ann Arbor, Michigan], July 23, 1863, Dexter Historical Society, Dexter, Michigan.

Chapter Seven
In Tribute to the Gallant 4th Michigan

The date was June 12, 1889. The place was Gettysburg. Not quite twenty-six years had passed since that fateful day in the Wheatfield, and Michigan, not unlike other northern states, had established a Gettysburg Battlefield Commission. The task of the commission was to raise funds and place monuments upon the field of battle where Michigan units distinguished themselves. On this day, approximately forty members of the 4th Michigan Volunteer Infantry gathered in the Wheatfield for the dedication of the 4th's monument which stands near the intersection of Rose's Woods and Stony Hill, where Colonel Jeffords lost his life trying to recapture and defend the regimental flag.[1]

The ceremony opened with the singing of "America" and concluded with "Nearer My God To Thee," two emotionally powerful songs, especially considering the circumstances. Between the two songs were two speeches and a poem. Excerpts of those proceedings written by members of the 4th Michigan Infantry provide an appropriate closure to this narrative. One is a quote by Capt. Lester H. Salsbury and the other is a poem by Bvt. Maj. Richard Watson Seage. Captain Salsbury was a sergeant with Company B at Gettysburg and was wounded in the Wheatfield. Brevet Major Seage was a second lieutenant with Company I and was severely wounded at the Wheatfield.[2]

In Captain Salsbury's words, "Eternal honor to that grand army of volunteers who here wrought out this grand consummation for us, and wrote its name high among the historic armies of the earth."[3]

Major Seage's tribute to his 4th Michigan Volunteer Infantry comrades follows:

---

1. Gettysburg Battlefield Commission, *Michigan at Gettysburg* (Detroit: Winn and Hammond, 1889), pp. 81-90.
2. *Ibid.*
3. *Ibid.*

Steve Roberts Collection

Veterans of the 4th Michigan

This group photograph of veterans of the 4th Michigan was taken on June 12, 1889, at the dedication of the regiment's monument, placed near the point where Colonel Harrison Jeffords lost his life by bayonet wound while attempting to recover the 4th's colors.

Poem Of
Brevet Major R. Watson Seage
June 12, 1889

The Army paused to rest awhile,
All hearts were light, each face a smile
And jokes went round through rank and file,
    We knew not then of Gettysburg.
Perchance a wit roused up, and then
Played the buffoon for graver men;
Nor dreamed we of the future, when
    The cloud should burst o'er Gettysburg.
A bugle sounds. "What means it! Say?"
A General Staff just passed this way.
Said one, - "I think we'll fight to-day,
    For Lee's in force at Gettysburg."
The veterans well knew what it meant
For Meade had re-enforcement sent
To Reynolds' men, now well nigh spent
    In holding ground at Gettysburg.
Our three days' march was nearly done;
Foot sore and scorched 'neath burning sun,
We waited now the signal gun;
    To take our turn in Gettysburg.
And presently there came a sound,
That filled the heavens and shook the ground,
And echoed wildly all around
    The woods and vales of Gettyburg.
"Fall in! Fall in!" The host uprose,
With one consent, to meet its foes;
Thus did the morning dawn for those
    Who fought with us, at Gettysburg.
What were our thoughts? - You ask in vain,
For scarcely two men felt the same;
Before us on the open plain--
    'Twas LIFE or DEATH at Gettysburg.
Some thought of HOME, and raised the prayer:
"Father, this day our firesides spare,
And if we fall, in mercy care
    For those bereft by Gettysburg."
And some with doubts and fears oppressed,
Others with thoughts of sin distressed,
And some said: "Comrades, Breast to Breast
    We'll stand or fall at Gettysburg."
Said Christian men: "We humbly pray,

O, God! for our success this day,
Help Thou the right, aid us to say
    Thy will be done at Gettysburg."
As on we hurried came the cry
Of battling hosts for victory;
"Unfurl Your Colors!" Let them fly
    To cheer the men at Gettysburg.
We pass by scores the Boys in Blue,
Jaded and sick and wounded, too,
They'll rest awhile, and then anew
    Fill up the Gaps in Gettysburg.
"Fresh Troops! Hurrah!" rings over the field,
Now to the North, the South must yield;
We knew them not; their hearts were steeled
    To WIN or DIE at Gettysburg.
This was the turning point, if won
By Southern arms their work was done.
Were ours the day, a Northern sun
    Would shine as now o'er Gettysburg.
The cannon roar from every mound,
And horsemen fly at bugle sound,
While wounded men upon the ground
    Were bruised and crushed at Gettysburg.
In ghastly heaps the dead were thrown;
In shapeless piles the wounded strewn;
Like fields of grain the men were mown
    By shot and shell at Gettysburg.
And still the carnage fierce grew,
And yet the fight fresh troops renew,
And more the murderous bullets flew,
    Laden with death at Gettysburg.
And still the strife throughout the day
Abates not 'tween the Blue and Gray,
At nightfall Thirty Thousand lay
    Upon the field of Gettysburg.
The end has come. Let those who bled
Be e'er revered as honored dead.
Let Peace her glorious mantle spread
    And hide from all men Gettysburg.
What of the Living? Were they not true
In time of need and danger, too?
They fought for Right, for Home, for You,
    And shunned not even Gettysburg.
Honor them well, Old Comrades Brave,

They did their best the land to save,
Wealthy or poor, their all they gave
    Before the guns at Gettysburg.
If then these sufferings made us free,
And gave our bond men Liberty,
We'll say: Thrice blessed the chastening be,
    And thank the Lord for Gettysburg.
Let us in unity to-day,
Lift up the prostrate foe and say
The Northern Blue and Southern Gray
    Brothers shall be since Gettysburg.
If well the PAST has been, or ill,
We have the glorious PRESENT still.
In FUTURE let us trust HIS will
    Who brought us safe through Gettysburg.
Comrades, we send a brother's cheer,
As you convene from far and near.
May this eclipse each former year
    In harmony since Gettysburg.
Live honest lives. Let every one
Be faithful till his time shall come,
Then heaven will surely "Welcome Home"
    Each Noble Son of Gettysburg.
"God of our sires." within whose hand
The Nations rest, "like grains of sand."
Bless Thou our great and glorious land
    Baptized in blood at Gettysburg.[4]

---

4. *Ibid.*

Chapter Eight
Michigan Veterans Assistance

The war was over but the effects upon the health of the combatants were long lasting. The federal government recognized this condition and established a network of national Old Soldiers' Homes in Augusta, Maine; Hampton, Virginia; Dayton, Ohio and Milwaukee, Wisconsin, to provide care for those physically or mentally impaired veterans. Within twenty years, Michigan began to consider the need to provide a state facility for veterans. It was not that the national homes were deficient in their services; rather, the demand for services far surpassed their capacity.[1]

In 1884, Michigan representatives and senators solicited the federal government for a home in Michigan as an extension of the national Old Soldiers' Home. The federal government failed to act on the associated bills. Efforts shifted to the state legislature, where, on June 5, 1885, Act No. 152 provided $100,000 for the establishment of a facility and $50,000 to maintain it during 1885 and 1886 and to provide services until the facility was completed. By June 3, 1886, the cornerstone was laid in the Soldiers' Home location north of Grand Rapids overlooking the Grand River. The facility was dedicated on December 30, 1886, and the doors opened on December 31, 1886.[2]

Through the course of the years, thirty-five veterans of the 4th Michigan and Reorganized 4th Michigan Infantry found their way to the home. Most of those veterans were buried in the home's military cemetery, originally laid out in the shape of a Maltese cross with a large monument at its center. Although the cemetery has expanded, the shape of the Maltese cross can still be discerned as the initial four burial sections are bordered by both paved and sunken dirt roads. Appendix Five includes photographs of headstones in this cemetery as well as short biographies of those soldiers who are buried there.[3]

1. *Michigan Veterans' Facility Centennial: A Century of Caring* (N.p.: West Michigan Printing, 1986), pp. 1-6.
2. *Ibid.*
3. *Ibid.*

Appendix One
Gettysburg Casualties

COMPANY A

Name and Gettysburg Rank	Status	Comments
French, Capt. Ebenezer	Wounded	Shot in arm
Brown, 1st Lt. William C.	Wounded	Shot in right side
Carney, Sgt. Simon B.	Captured	Died of disease in prison
Lassey, Sgt. Richard R.	Captured	Died of tonsillitis in prison
Paul, Sgt. George W.	Captured	Paroled Nov. 1864
Benson, Cpl. Adelbert	Killed	Buried near Rose's Barn
Ladd, Cpl. Charles H.	Killed	Buried near Rose's Barn
Laird, Cpl. David C.	Wounded	Died of wounds, Nov. 1863
Olson, Cpl. Martin	Captured	Died, Richmond prison, Sept. 27, 1863
Robinson, Cpl. Henry	Wounded	Shot in the back
Whipple, Cpl. George G.	Captured	Died of disease, Andersonville
Ansel, Pvt. Henry I.	Wounded	Aided other wounded
Baker, Pvt. John F.	Wounded	Shot in right hip and left arm
Bisonette, Pvt. Samuel	Killed	Buried near Rose's Barn
Davidson, Pvt. Augustus	Missing	Captured, returned to regt., 1864
Disher, Pvt. John	Captured	Returned to regt., Oct. 9, 1863
Olney, Pvt. George W.	Captured	Died in prison
Regal, Pvt. Isaiah	Wounded	Shot in arm; trans. to Invalid Corps
Scranton, Pvt. Alphonso	Missing	Returned to regt., 1864
Spath, Pvt. Frederick	Wounded	Trans. to Invalid Corps
Thurlack, Pvt. Charles	Killed	Buried near Rose's Barn
Whipple, Pvt. George M.	Captured	Died of disease, Andersonville

COMPANY B

Name and Gettysburg Rank	Status	Comments
Barrett, 2nd Lt. Orvey S.	Wounded	Shot in left leg; discharged
Day, 2nd Lt. Adelbert F.	Wounded	Returned to regt., Sept. 1863
Kimball, Sgt. Duane C.	Wounded	Leg amputated; died of wounds
Salsbury, Sgt. Lester H.	Wounded	Shot in hand, left thigh and lung; discharged
Bellows, Cpl. Alonzo C.	Wounded	Shot in right leg
Dirdbess, Cpl. George W.	Wounded	Shot in both thighs
Millens, Cpl. George W.	Captured	Died at Andersonville, 1864
Young, Cpl. George E.	Captured	

Name	Status	Comments
Brockway, Pvt. Martin	Captured	Released 1865
Burce, Pvt. Joseph	Wounded	
Langford, Daniel W.	Captured	Returned to regt., Aug. 1863
Lewis, Pvt. Alonzo	Wounded	Shot in right leg
Lewis, Pvt. Edward	Killed	
Partridge, Pvt. Leonard	Wounded	Shot in leg
Tasker, Pvt. Richard	Captured	Returned to regt., Sept. 1863
Warne, Pvt. Harvey	Captured	Died in prison, 1864
Warner, Pvt. Harvey L.	Captured	Taken prisoner three times
Wheaton, Pvt. Andrew	Wounded	Shot below the knee
Williams, Pvt. George	Captured	Returned to regt., Sept. 1863

COMPANY C

Name and Gettysburg Rank	Status	Comments
Rickett, Sgt. Don A.	Wounded	Shot through the back
Mills, Cpl. Almyron	Captured	
Pease, Cpl. Constantine	Wounded	Shot in hip; died of wounds
Worden, Cpl. Freeman P.	Killed	Buried near Rose's Barn
Beal, Pvt. Henry E.	Wounded	Shot in right shoulder
Bird, Pvt. James M.	Captured	Died in prison
Blanchard, Pvt. Wm. H.	Captured	Returned to regt. Nov. 20, 1864
Cooper, Pvt. William B.	Wounded	Shot in head with buckshot
Cowgill, Pvt. Cyrenius C.	Captured	Died at Richmond Prison, Feb. 2, 1864
Crain, Pvt. John F.	Wounded	
David, Pvt. Orson	Killed	
Dudley, Pvt. David T.	Captured	Returned to regt., Nov. 9, 1863
Enos, Pvt. Merritt	Captured	Returned to regt., Jan. 1, 1864
Flera, Pvt. James C.	Wounded	Shot in left ankle
Halstead, Pvt. Frank G.	Captured	Returned to regt., Nov. 14, 1864
Hoagland, Pvt. Franklin	Captured	Died at Richmond prison, Oct. 24, 1863
Kidney, Pvt. John P.	Wounded	Shot in left shoulder
Mills, Pvt. Charles	Captured	Returned to regt., Oct. 1863
Mohorther, Pvt. Charles	Wounded	Trans. to Invalid Corps
Powell, Pvt. Benjamin W.	Captured	Died at Richmond prison, Sept. 15, 1863
Sargent, Pvt. John	Captured	Escaped from Andersonville, 1864
Skirvin, Pvt. Charles M.	Wounded	
Thompson, Pvt. Wesley J.	Captured	Paroled, August 1863
Thurston, Pvt. Epaminonda	Wounded	

COMPANY D

Name and Gettysburg Rank	Status	Comments
Sheets, Sgt. Frederick A.	Wounded	Shot in leg and arm; died of wounds
Smith, Sgt. Oliver S.	Captured	Returned to regt., Nov. 1863
King, Cpl. Norman	Killed	
Phelps, Cpl. Charles W.	Killed	
Pryor, Cpl. William A.	Killed	
Whitmore, Cpl. Lewis F.	Killed	

Name	Status	Comments
Zimmerman, Cpl. Dions	Killed	
Bauer, Pvt. Anton	Wounded	Shot in left arm; trans. to Invalid Corps
Bensler, Pvt. Jacob	Wounded	Shot in right shoulder by shell
Comstock, Pvt. Ellis B.	Killed	
Cook, Pvt. Jacob F.	Captured	Returned to regt., July 2, 1864
Crawford, Pvt. Quimby	Wounded	Shot right side of head
Cronenwill, Pvt. William	Wounded	Shot in left leg; trans. to Invalid Corps
Dates, Pvt. John J.	Wounded	Shot in left thigh; discharged
Dexter, Pvt. Flavius J.	Captured	Returned to regt., Nov. 9, 1863
Hudler, Pvt. James M.	Wounded	Shot in ankle; discharged
Hughes, Pvt. George L.	Wounded	Shot in left ankle; discharged
Lynch, Pvt. William	Missing	Presumed dead
Marshall, Pvt. George E.	Captured	Died at Richmond prison, 1864
Rouse, Pvt. Charles A.	Killed	
Smith, Pvt. Washington	Missing	Presumed dead
Silsby, Pvt. James P.	Captured	
Webster, Pvt. David	Captured	Returned to regt., Nov. 1864

COMPANY E

Name and Gettysburg Rank	Status	Comments
Ainsworth, Cpl. Riley N.	Captured	Died at Richmond prison
Lake, Cpl. Amon C.	Wounded	Shot in thigh; died of wounds
Pennock, Cpl. Martin V.	Captured	Died of disease at Richmond prison
Taylor, Cpl. Edward M.	Wounded	Shot in leg
Best, Pvt. Benjamin	Wounded	Shot in the toe
Burnett, Pvt. Chauncey	Wounded	Shot in shoulder
Burtch, Pvt. Thomas B.	Captured	
Coffin, Pvt. Seth D.	Wounded	Shot in arm
Fleming, Pvt. John	Wounded	Taken prisoner
Fuller, Pvt. William	Captured	Richmond prison
Huff, Pvt. Thaddeus	Wounded	Shot in leg
Perine, Pvt. Jacob H.	Wounded	Shot in thigh
Stacey, Pvt. George H.	Wounded	
Stanback, Pvt. Philip	Wounded	Shot in arm
Tarsney, Pvt. John	Captured	
Taylor, Pvt. Mark W.	Wounded	Discharged
Walker, Pvt. George A.	Wounded	Died of wounds
Ward, Pvt. George T.	Wounded	Shot in leg and thigh
Ward, Pvt. Gilbert D.	Wounded	Shot in thigh; discharged

COMPANY F

Name and Gettysburg Rank	Status	Comments
Westfall, Lt. Benjamin	Wounded	Shot in right hand
Brownell, Sgt. John	Captured	Died of starvation in prison
Fountain, Sgt. Hiram B.	Killed	Buried near Rose's Barn
Goodsell, Sgt. George A.	Wounded	Served in Color Company
Lenbocker, Sgt. Wm. E.	Captured	Shot and killed in prison
Clark, Cpl. Frank	Wounded	Shot in head and leg; leg amputated

Name	Status	Comments
Coville, Cpl. Andrew	Missing	Presumed dead
Gue, Cpl. Leonard L.	Wounded	Shot in arm; trans. to Invalid Corps
Johnson, Cpl. Freeman	Missing	Wounded; trans. to Invalid Corps
Miner, Cpl. Ervin S.	Captured	Wounded; trans. to Invalid Corps
Smith, Cpl. Albert	Wounded	Missing and presumed dead
Bois, Pvt. Albert H.	Wounded	Shot in hand; trans. to Invalid Corps
Dillon, Pvt. William B.	Captured	Died in Richmond prison, Dec. 25, 1865
Doty, Pvt. Orasmus M.	Wounded	Taken prisoner
Hamlin, Pvt. Edgar V.	Missing	
Hamlin, Pvt. Royal W.	Wounded	Returned to regt., Aug. 1864
Hassington, Pvt. Addison	Killed	Buried near Rose's Barn
Heath, Pvt. Chauncy	Captured	Returned to regt., March 1864
Lewis, Pvt. George W.	Wounded	Shot in arm; trans. to Invalid Corps
Westfall, Pvt. Charles J.	Wounded	Shot in arm

COMPANY G

Name and Gettysburg Rank	Status	Comments
Curtis, Sgt. Ambrose	Wounded	Shot in foot
Morgan, Cpl. Moses	Wounded	Shot in thigh
Eastick, Pvt. Newman A.	Captured	Died in *Sultana* disaster
Hendershot, Pvt. Wm.	Missing	
Hoagland, Pvt. Thomas	Captured	
Mackey, Pvt. John H.	Wounded	Shot in foot
Owen, Pvt. Andrew	Missing	
Pennock, Pvt. Alonzo	Missing	
Plummer, Pvt. Wm. H.	Wounded	Shot in thigh
Walters, Pvt. Erastus	Wounded	Shot in thigh
Whelan, Pvt. Edwin M.	Captured	

COMPANY H

Name and Gettysburg Rank	Status	Comments
Robinson, Capt. Wm. F.	Wounded	Shot in leg; discharged
Walker, Lt. Samuel G.	Wounded	Shot in left arm
Tripp, Sgt. Edwin G.	Wounded	Shot in both legs; died of wounds
Willis, Sgt. Sidney	Captured	Escaped
LaFleur, Cpl. Asher B.	Wounded	
Stilwell, Cpl. James I.	Captured	
Ashmore, Pvt. Obed S.	Captured	
Bennett, Pvt. Alexander	Captured	Died in prison
Brink, Pvt. Joseph	Killed	
Brown, Pvt. John	Wounded	Shot in shoulder and hand; died of wounds
Gregery, Pvt. Charles W.	Killed	Buried near Rose's Barn
Hamp, Pvt. Clark G.	Wounded	
Hardy, Pvt. John D.	Wounded	Shot through leg
Lazilier, Pvt. George	Wounded	Shot in arm and shoulder
Pendelton, Pvt. James H.	Killed	

Name and Gettysburg Rank	Status	Comments
Purdy, Pvt. George	Killed	
Wilson, Pvt. Charles	Wounded	Shot in left lung; died of wounds
Yawger, Pvt. Chester S.	Captured	

COMPANY I

Name and Gettysburg Rank	Status	Comments
Seage, 2nd Lt. R. Watson	Wounded	Shot in chest and arm; discharged
Vreeland, Lt. Michael J.	Wounded	Shot in hand and chest
Fenton, Sgt. James	Captured	Died of wounds
Eliot, Sgt. Elmer	Missing	
Jackson, Sgt. William H.	Killed	
Kydd, Sgt. John	Killed	Buried in Rose's Woods
Loss, Cpl. Charles P.	Captured	
Phelps, Cpl. Burton L.	Wounded	Discharged
Allen, Pvt. William H.	Captured	
Lapham, Pvt. George	Killed	
Davis, Pvt. James	Captured	
Haight, Pvt. Daniel M.	Wounded	
Harrington, Pvt. Erastus	Missing	Presumed dead
Hutchins, Pvt. George	Killed	
Jehu, Pvt. David	Wounded	Died enroute to hospital
Kruger, Pvt. Christian B.	Wounded	
Moore, Pvt. John B.	Missing	Presumed dead
Rose, Pvt. Myron	Wounded	Trans. to Invalid Corps
Saliotte, Pvt. Gilbert	Captured	
Smith, Pvt. James P.	Wounded	Trans. to Invalid Corps
Wilsey, Pvt. Henry	Captured	Died in prison, Jan., 1864
Wilsey, Pvt. Jeremiah	Captured	Released March 13, 1865

COMPANY K

Name and Gettysburg Rank	Status	Comments
Jeffords, Col. Harrison H.	Wounded	Died of bayonet wound
McLean, Capt. James B.	Wounded	Discharged
Brown, Sgt. Ezra	Wounded	
Hyatt, Cpl. James E.	Wounded	
Gahagan, Pvt. Peter	Wounded	Died of wounds
Johnson, Pvt. James	Killed	
Kellogg, Pvt. E. Lyman	Captured	
Lampman, Pvt. Lawson	Killed	
Lumbard, Pvt. Horatio G.	Captured	Taken to Libby prison
Moodie, Pvt. Robert	Wounded	Shot in back; died of wounds
Storms, Pvt. Abram W.	Missing	

Appendix Two
Roster of the 4th Michigan Volunteer Infantry

STAFF[1]

Name	Enlistment Rank	Age	End of Service	Remarks
Woodbury, Dwight A.	Colonel	36	July 1862	Killed in action
Duffield, William	Lt. Colonel	22	Jan. 1862	Disability
Childs, Johnathan W.	Major	28	Nov. 1862	Hon. discharge
Earle, Francis S.	Adjutant	24	Sept. 1862	Transferred
Lamson, Alvan C.	Sgt. Maj.	22	April 1864	
Grannis, Henry A.	Qtrm.	32	Nov. 1862	Hon. discharge
Reeve, Selah V.	Qtrm. Sgt.	27	Sept. 1861	Transferred
Tunnicliff, Joseph W.	Surgeon	42	Aug. 1861	Transferred
Chamberlain, David P.	Asst. Surg.	37	Feb. 1863	Hon. Discharge
Harrington, Jerome F.	Steward	26	Sept. 1861	Transferred
Strong, Henry N.	Chaplain	35	July 1862	Hon. discharge

COMPANY A

Name	Enlistment Rank	Age	End of Service	Remarks
Luce, Constant	Capt.	40	Nov. 1861	Disability
Oliver, John M.	First Lt.	33	Mar. 1863	Transferred
Rose, A. Morrell	Second Lt.	29	July 1862	Killed
Spaulding, Geo. W.	First Sgt.	24	July 1862	Transferred
Bradford, George W.	Sergeant	23	Nov. 1862	Transferred
Paulding, Cornelius	Sergeant	20	Aug. 1861	Died of disease
Redfield, James	Sergeant	21	Sept. 1862	Disability
Bowen, Adna H.	Corporal	19	Mar. 1863	Transferred
Brimingstoll, Horace	Corporal	18	June 1864	
Brown, William C.	Corporal	32	June 1864	
Gale, Frank B.	Corporal	19	July 1862	Killed in action
Kendall, Harry	Corporal	19	Oct. 1861	Died of disease
Lassey, Richard R.	Corporal	28	Dec. 1863	Died in prison
Paulding, Willis G.	Corporal	22	Feb. 1862	Disability
Stodard, Herbert L.	Corporal	21	Sept. 1861	
Chooted, George	Musician	22	June 1864	
Ansel, Henry		19	June 1864	

1. Unless otherwise noted, all members of the 4th Michigan listed herein were mustered in June, 1863.

Name	Age	Date	Notes
Austin, Charles F.	21	July 1862	Killed in action
Baker, Newell E.	19	Oct. 1861	Disability
Beaman, George W.	19	June 1864	
Benderitter, Frank	19	June 1864	
Benson, Aldebert	19	July 1863	
Billings, Edgar M.	23	Feb. 1866	
Bisbee, Charles E.	19	Oct. 1862	Disability
Bisonette, Samuel	22	July 1863	Killed in action
Bronson, Edward	29	Mar. 1864	Disability
Brunner, Charles	19	May 1864	Died of wounds
Bussins, John	22	Feb. 1866	
Carney, Simon B.	24	Nov. 1863	Died of disease
Cauchie, William	30	Nov. 1862	Trans. to Ambulance Corps
Chapman, Jonathan		June 1865	
Charter, Jackson	22	June 1864	
Chase, James F.	20	June 1864	
Cicott, Elvi	35	Feb. 1863	Disability
Cicso, Lorenzo	20	July 1861	Disability
Coulan, John	23	June 1864	
Coutre, Samuel S.	27	Nov. 1862	
Curtiss, Benjamin F.	19	June 1864	
Dickinson, John R.	25	June 1864	
Disher, John	19	July 1865	
Downing, Christopher	20	Nov. 1863	Disability
Duffield, Johnson	20	June 1864	
Eaton, William H.	20	July 1862	Killed in action
Fonier, John B.	28	July 1862	Killed in action
Gibson, William H.	25	June 1864	
Godfroy, Frederick	19	June 1861	Disability
Gonier, Xavier	29	June 1864	
Grannison, George	22	Nov. 1862	Transferred
Graviot, Hiram	20	July 1861	Disability
Guior, Andrew		July 1862	Disability
Guior, Kibbie	25		Unknown discharge
Haberfelder, Theodor	19	May 1863	Killed in action
Hall, Mifflin	35	June 1864	
Harmon, Frederick	20	Sept. 1861	Died of disease
Heald, James	32	June 1864	
Henerson, David	24	July 1862	Transferred
Hinsdale, James W.	19	Feb. 1866	
Hoffman, Frederick	24	May 1863	Killed in action
Kempt, Godfrey	23	June 1865	
Kidder, Samuel C.	20	Sept. 1861	Transferred
Kittle, Jesse	22	July 1862	Killed in action
Knaggs, Wesley J.	22	Nov. 1862	Disability due to wounds
Knape, August	25	July 1862	Killed in action
Kronbach, Adam		June 1864	
Ladd, Charles H.	23	July 1863	Killed in action
Laird, David	19	Dec. 1863	Died of wounds
Lassey, William	19	June 1864	
Leonard, Freeman	22	July 1862	Died of disease
Leonard, John	18	Feb. 1863	Died of disease
Mosier, Aaron	22	July 1862	Killed in action

Name	Age		Remarks
Mosier, Isaac	42	Dec. 1861	Disability
Navarre, Isaac	20	July 1862	Killed in action
Nelson, Benjamin F.	22	June 1864	
Nolan, Thomas	19	Feb. 1862	Transferred
Olney, George W.	19	June 1864	Died in prison
Olson, Martin	26	Oct. 1863	Died in prison
Owen, George W.	21	Feb. 1866	
Parker, Sewell S.	20	Sept. 1862	Transferred
Paul, George D.	30	Jan. 1865	
Pence, William H.	30	Jan. 1865	Disability
Pluse, Sherman D.	21	Nov. 1862	Disability due to wounds
Pordon, John	23	Feb. 1866	
Roberts, John B.	21	Mar. 1865	Disability due to wounds
Robinson, Henry	21	June 1864	
Root, Jason	19	June 1864	
Spath, Frederick	20	Sept. 1863	Trans. to Invalid Corps
Stewart, William S.	23	July 1862	Disability
Stoddard, Edgar C.	19	Sept. 1861	
Suzor, Joseph	20	April 1863	Disability
Taylor, Addison A.	19	June 1864	
Taylor, Edward H.	21	June 1864	
Teachout, Charles	19	July 1862	Killed in action
Thurlack, Charles	22	July 1863	Killed in Action
Turner, James H.	20	June 1864	
Villett, Charles		Mar. 1863	Disability
Wagner, Levi	20	Oct. 1861	Disability
Walters, John	19	July 1862	Killed in action
Watkins, William H.	20	Dec. 1862	Killed in action
Watson, Clarke	25	July 1862	Killed in action
Watson, William C.	25	June 1864	
Wells, Charles	21	Aug. 1862	Died of wounds
Whipple, George G.		April 1864	Died in prison
Woodward, Edward	20	June 1865	
Yates, George H.	22	June 1864	

COMPANY B

Name	Enlistment Rank	Age	End of Service	Remarks
Cole, James H.	Captain	24	July 1862	Disability
Hamm, Richard P.	First Lt.		Aug. 1861	Resigned
Avery, James E.	Second Lt.	28	Dec. 1862	Hon. Discharge
Battey, William F.	First Sgt.	23	Sept. 1861	Disability
Barrett, Orvey S.	Sergeant	26	May 1864	Disability, wounds
Jones, Thomas D.	Sergeant	23	July 1862	Died of wounds
Rintz, John	Sergeant	24	May 1866	
Williams, Harmon G.	Sergeant	24	Dec. 1861	Deserted
Albion, James R.	Corporal	25	Sept. 1863	Trans. to Invalid Corps
Canfield, Alfred E.	Corporal	21	Feb. 1862	Disability
Jones, Timothy T.	Corporal	21	July 1865	

Name	Rank	Age	Date	Remarks
Kimball, Duane C.	Corporal	18	July 1863	Died of wounds
Rollins, Charles	Corporal	26	Sept. 1861	Disability
Salsbury, Lester H.	Corporal	21	Jan. 1864	Disability, wounds
Shafer, Alphonzo	Corporal	21	Feb. 1866	
Nichols, Henry	Musician	36	Feb. 1866	
Tenbrook, Wm. L.	Musician	22	Feb. 1866	
Springstead, J. A.	Wagoner	23	April 1864	Disability
Adair, James H.		22	June 1864	
Aldrich, Eugene		19	Sept. 1861	Disability
Allen, Charles		22	June 1864	
Atkinson, Theodore P.		25	June 1862	Killed in action
Bailey, Jared B.		21	Jan. 1862	Disability
Baker, William F.		19	Jan. 1863	Disability
Barnes, Dexter C.		31	Mar. 1862	Disability
Barnes, Lewis		21	June 1862	Killed in action
Bates, Charles		19	Sept. 1861	Disability
Bellows, Alonzo C.		24	June 1864	
Bender, David		23	Feb. 1866	
Bently, Jonathan		33	Oct. 1861	Disability
Bixler, Frank M.		21	Mar. 1864	Disability
Britton, William		21	Jan. 1862	Disability
Brockway, Martin		26	July 1865	
Bryon, Joseph		24	Feb. 1866	
Burns, Edward C.		22	Feb. 1865	
Campbell, John E.		35	Jan. 1864	Disability, wounds
Carpenter, Washington		21	June 1864	
Carver, Orville		19	June 1864	
Caswell, Andrew D.		24	April 1863	Disability
Crocket, Leroy		18	Sept. 1861	Died of disease
Croxton, Lafayette J.		21	Oct. 1862	Disability, wounds
Culver, Adelbert D.		19	Sept. 1862	Disability, wounds
Daley, Michael		21	Jan. 1863	Disability, wounds
Davis, Enoch		25	May 1864	Killed in action
Day, Aldebert F.		18	Sept. 1865	
Dirdbess, George W.		21	June 1864	
Drake, Franklin		19	May 1862	Died of wounds
Duncan, Charles S.		23	June 1864	
Easlick, William		22	Jan. 1862	Disability
Evans, James		19	Jan. 1863	Disability
Farrar, Dewitt C.		22	Dec. 1862	Killed in action
Fisher, Homer E.		21	Jan. 1863	Disability
Fitch, Edson J.		19	June 1864	
Foote, Emery		23	Feb. 1866	
Fuller, Orson		18	Sept. 1861	Disability
Garnsey, Albert L.		22	Feb. 1866	
Garnsey, Roswell L.		21	June 1862	Killed in action
Gilleland, James G.		21	June 1864	
Hackett, Andrew		21	June 1864	
Harrison, William H.		31	May 1864	Died of wounds
Kemery, Absalom		28	Dec. 1861	Disability
Kingsley, Andrew J.		31	Mar. 1862	Disability

Name	Age	Date	Remarks
Langford, Daniel W.	25	Oct. 1864	Died in prison
Lockwood, Elias	21	Nov. 1863	
Maples, Andrus	21	Feb. 1866	
McBride, Quintus J.	21	Aug. 1861	Died of disease
McDougall, James	38	Jan. 1862	Died of disease
Meech, Frederick W.	24	June 1862	Killed in action
Meek, David	24	Feb. 1866	
Millens, Cyrus	25	April 1863	Disability
Millins, George W.	22	Feb. 1864	Died in prison
Morse, Sanford	22	Feb. 1866	
Munger, Thomas	21	June 1862	Killed in action
Myer, George	25	Feb. 1863	Disability, wounds
Partridge, Leonard	21	Feb. 1866	
Patrick, Alexander L.	24	June 1864	
Perkins, Marion D.	18	May 1863	Missing
Pier, William D. F.	25	Jan. 1863	Disability
Pierce, William J.	22	Dec. 1861	Died of disease
Piper, Abel M. D.	24	May 1862	Killed in action
Piper, Alanson R.	18	Mar. 1866	
Priest, George	21	Mar. 1863	Disability
Priest, Mathias	22	Jan. 1863	Disability
Richardson, John	24	Aug. 1862	Disability, wounds
Riley, Philip	23	Feb. 1866	
Shafer, Alexander	19	Feb. 1866	
Shick, Charles	21	April 1862	Disability
Sperry, Alfred E.	21	April 1863	Died of disease
Tasker, Richard	22	June 1864	Died of wounds
Taylor, David	21	Nov. 1862	Transferred
Tichnor, Henry	19	Sept. 1865	
Tillotson, George	25	Feb. 1865	Killed in action
Warner, Harvey L.	27	Aug. 1864	Died of wounds
Wells, James H.	19	Feb. 1866	
Wheaton, Andrew	22	June 1864	
White, Johnson	19	Mar. 1864	Transferred
White, Newell	21	April 1863	Disability
Wiley, James	24	Sept. 1861	Died of disease
Williams, George	22	Feb. 1866	
Woodfield, Nathaniel	35	Oct. 1861	Disability
Wright, William D.	25	May 1864	Killed in action
Young, George E.	21	June 1864	

COMPANY C

Name	Enlistment Rank	Age	End of Service	Remarks
Wood, Abram R.	Captain	34	April 1862	Killed in action
French, Ebenezer	Second Lt.	26	May 1864	Disability
Gruner, Charles F.	First Sgt.	24	Aug. 1864	
Ainsley, George	Sergeant	20	July 1861	Disability
Bates, Gordon	Sergeant	20	June 1862	Disability
McCollister, Charles E.	Sergeant	24	June 1862	Disability
Starr, Eli L.	Sergeant	21	July 1862	Killed in action
Vesey, James W.	Sergeant	18	June 1864	Died of wounds

Name	Rank	Age	Date	Fate
Farr, Andrew J.	Corporal	25	June 1862	Killed in action
Fox, John W.	Corporal	21	April 1862	Died of disease
Kennedy, John	Corporal	27		Disability
McAfee, John	Corporal	19	June 1864	
Pease, Constantine	Corporal	20	Aug. 1863	Died in prison
Piersons, James	Corporal	22	Oct. 1862	Disability
Spellman, Frank	Corporal	19	July 1862	Killed in action
Vaugn, Eugene	Corporal	24	June 1864	
Garvin, Eugene	Musician	23	June 1864	
Whittlesy, Thomas B.	Musician	20	June 1864	
Kilmer, Alonzo	Wagoner	21	June 1864	
Akers, George W.		21	Mar. 1863	Disability
Anderson, Findlatur C.		20	Nov. 1861	Disability
Andrews, John		21	July 1862	Died of wounds
Barnes, Luke		21	June 1864	
Beal, Henry E.		31	June 1864	
Becker, Wilson		23	Dec. 1862	Killed in action
Bird, James M.		25	Dec. 1863	Died in prison
Blanchard, William		19	Mar. 1865	
Braman, William		24	June 1864	
Brigham, Lucian V.		34	June 1864	
Burr, James D.		18	June 1864	
Carnes, Charles F.		21	Oct. 1862	Disability
Carpenter, Adison I.		22	June 1864	
Chandler, George A.		43	Jan. 1865	
Chase, William H.		24	Oct. 1862	Disability
Cherry, William		26	Sept. 1861	Disability
Clay, Samuel		24	June 1862	Disability
Collins, George		18	July 1861	Deserted
Cook, George		21	June 1864	
Cooper, William B.		18	June 1864	
Cowgill, Cyrenius C.		23	Feb. 1864	Died in prison
Crain, John F.			June 1865	Deserted
Crain, Samuel		21		Unknown discharge
Cummings, William		22	Jan. 1862	Died of disease
Darrow, Joseph		27	Nov. 1862	Disability
David, Orson		21	July 1863	Killed in action
Dudley, David T.		22	June 1864	
Enos, Merritt		18	June 1864	
Fidler, Wesley D.		22	June 1864	
Field, Nelson			July 1861	
Fisk, Canfield		21	June 1864	
Flera, James C.		29	June 1864	
Flint, Lewis L.		21	Oct. 1863	Disability
Fry, Mahlon		18	Oct. 1863	
Fuller, Samuel		22	Jan. 1864	Died of disease
Goodrich, George W.		18	April 1863	Disability
Green, James S.		20	June 1864	
Halstead, Frank G.		22	Mar. 1863	
Harris, William			June 1861	Discharged
Hart, Lewis		20	Oct. 1862	Disability
Havens, Truman		39	Dec. 1862	Discharged
Hoagland, Franklin		22	Oct. 1863	Died in prison
Holcomb, William H.		25	Feb. 1863	Died of wounds

Name	Age	Date	Remarks
Hooker, W. H.		Dec. 1862	Died
Horner, John A.	18	Feb. 1863	
Howk, Fayette	28	April 1863	Disability
Hurlburt, Thomas J.	18	June 1865	
Hutt, Myron D.	21	June 1864	
Itzkins, George	18	Dec. 1862	Transferred
Kaizer, Andrew Jackson	20	June 1864	
Ketchum, Alvah	19	June 1864	
Kidney, John P.	23	June 1864	
Latta, Martin M.	21	Dec. 1862	Died of disease
Law, Charles E.		July 1862	Disability
Lee, George H.	23	Dec. 1862	Disability
Livinston, James	19	Feb. 1863	Disability
Low, Henry	21	July 1862	Died of wounds
Mann, Chauncey L.	22	June 1864	
McDonough, Michael	21	Oct. 1863	Trans. to Invalid Corps
Melville, William H.	19	Mar. 1864	
Mills, Almyron	19	June 1864	
Mills, Charles	21	June 1864	
Mohorter, Charles	21	Jan. 1864	Trans. to Invalid Corps
Parker, Philo C.	20	June 1862	Killed in action
Parsons, Alexus B.	43	July 1861	Died of disease
Powell, Benjamin W.	20	Sept. 1863	Died in prison
Price, Joseph	32	July 1862	Died of wounds
Rickett, Don A.	23	June 1864	
Rockwell, James K.	21		Trans. to Invalid Corps
Roupp, Jacob	32		Trans. to Invalid Corps
Sargent, John	21	Oct. 1864	
Schaffer, Albert	21	June 1862	Disability
Schaffer, Lewis	31	Nov. 1861	Died of disease
Scott, John D.	21	June 1864	
Skirvin, Marion	18	June 1864	
Stephens, William H.	18	Sept. 1861	Disability
Storms, James H.	26	Oct. 1861	Disability
Thomas, John	21	April 1862	Disability
Thompson, Wesley J.	18	June 1865	
Thurston, Epaminaonda	21	July 1865	
Tompkins, Joseph W.	30	July 1862	Disability
Tompson, James H.	19		No record
Toupance, Chester	18	Feb. 1866	
Vanguilder, Orrin	21	Dec. 1862	Transferred
Vanzant, Oliver	21	June 1864	
Wademan, Charles H.	18	June 1864	
Williams, George	18	Aug. 1862	Died of disease
Worden, Freeman P.	29	July 1863	Killed in action
Worden, Herman B.		June 1864	
Wyant, John W.	18	May 1863	Killed in action
Youngs, Jerome B.	22	Jan. 1864	Trans. to Invalid Corps

COMPANY D

Name	Enlistment Rank	Age	End of Service	Remarks
Randolf, John M.	Captain	34	May 1863	Disability
De Puy, Richard G.	First Lt.	30	June 1862	Killed in action
Hall, Jarius W.	2nd Lt.	21	May 1866	
Baldwin, Edward C.	Com. Sgt.	24	July 1863	Honorable discharge
Gilbert, Edwin H.	First Sgt.	22	June 1864	
Beach, Edward E.	Sergeant	23	June 1862	Disability
Hill, Henry G.	Sergeant	23	June 1864	
Loveland, William H.	Sergeant	21	May 1864	Died of wounds
Sheets, Frederick A.	Sergeant	42	July 1863	Died of wounds
Clark, James E.	Corporal	19	Dec. 1862	Killed in action
Davis, Hiram H.	Corporal	21	Jan. 1864	Trans. to Invalid Corps
Gates, John A.	Corporal	21	Oct. 1862	
Goodhue, Elmer	Corporal	24	July 1862	Killed in action
Mowry, Granville G.	Corporal	23	June 1864	
Richardson, Jonas D.	Corporal	21	Sept. 1863	Trans. to Invalid Corps
Truair, Frank B.	Corporal	27	Aug. 1863	Trans. to Invalid Corps
Ward, Joseph L.	Corporal	35	July 1862	Killed in action
Cranell, William W.	Musician	23	Aug. 1861	Disability
Andrews, John F.	Wagoner		July 1862	Deserted
Adams, William C.		23	Dec. 1861	Disability
Aldrich, Stephen H.		22	Dec. 1864	
Anderson, John F.		23	July 1862	Killed in action
Andrews, Charles L.		23	Oct. 1862	
Bacon, Reuben C.		23	Jan. 1864	Disability
Bardwell, George W.		24	Nov. 1861	Deserted
Bartlett, John		46	Mar. 1862	Disability
Bauer, Anton		27	Feb. 1864	Trans. to Invalid Corps
Beckley, Guy		31	Sept. 1861	Disability
Besemer, Charles B.		34	Dec. 1864	
Bliss, Edmund		21	Sept. 1863	Trans. to Invalid Corps
Boyd, Thomas		22	June 1864	
Bryant, Martin V.		24	Nov. 1862	Disability
Comstock, Chester W.		23	Sept. 1865	Disability
Comstock, John W.		25	Feb. 1866	
Cranston, Robert H.		19	Jan. 1864	
Crawford, Quimby H.		19	June 1864	
Cronenwill, William H.		24	Jan. 1864	Trans. to Invalid Corps
Dates, John J.		40	Jan. 1864	Disability, wounds
Dean, Charles B.		23	Feb. 1863	Transferred
Dean, Eli H.		22	July 1862	Killed in action
Denman, William		22	May 1862	Disability
Dexter, Flavius J.		21	June 1864	
Donnelly, Alexander		23	Sept. 1861	Disability
Dutton, Henry		22	Jan. 1862	Disability

Name	Age	Date	Status
Fisher, John	18	Feb. 1863	Disability, wounds
Goodrich, Morrell	42	July 1862	Disability
Gradener, Charles	28	Jan. 1864	Disability
Harley, Jonathan P.	25	Nov. 1862	
Hudler, James M.	29	May 1864	Disability, wounds
Hurd, Lewis G.	21	Mar. 1862	Killed in action
Huxford, William P.	19		Disability, wounds
Jackson, Joseph		Aug. 1861	Died of disease
Keedle, James	23	Sept. 1864	
Keeler, Lewis W.	26	Feb. 1866	
King, Norman	22	July 1863	Killed in action
Knowing, Edward		Oct. 1861	Died of disease
Lowe, David	31	May 1864	Killed in action
Lynch, William	24	July 1863	Missing in action
Mason, Miles T.	22	June 1864	
McCormick, Charles	21	Feb. 1863	Disability
McFadden, Michael	23	Feb. 1865	
McKenzine, William	27	June 1864	
Morse, Birdsey H.	23	Oct. 1862	
Murphy, James H.	22	Feb. 1866	
Newton, Henry W.	18	May 1863	Killed in action
Newton, Thomas W.	43	Feb. 1866	
Null, Henry	24	Nov. 1862	Disability
Parkhurst, Abel	34	Sept. 1862	Disability
Patrick, George	21	Sept. 1861	Disability
Perry, Edwin S.	27	Feb. 1866	
Phelps, Charles W.	21	July 1863	Killed in action
Piquet, Peter	25	Nov. 1862	
Pomeroy, Charles	29	Dec. 1862	Disability
Pryor, William A.	26	July 1863	Killed in action
Reeves, Charles	28	May 1862	Killed in action
Ritter, Lewis	23	Mar. 1863	Disability
Rouse, Charles A.	19	July 1863	Killed in action
Rozell, Daniel R.	20	Nov. 1862	Disability, wounds
Saunders, John	35	June 1864	
Sayers, Frank	21	Nov. 1862	Disability
Shaw, Gilmore M.	21		Hospitalized; no further record
Showers, Andrew J.	22	Nov. 1862	
Silsby, Frederick R.	24	Aug. 1863	
Silsby, James P.	24	Jan. 1865	
Smith, Oliver S.	22	Jan. 1865	Transferred
Smith, Washington E.	26	July 1863	Missing
Spencer, Tenant R.	29	1862	Died of disease
Stevens, Nelson	21	Dec. 1861	Disability
Sweet, William	34	Nov. 1862	Disability
Taylor, William J.	23	Nov. 1862	Disability
Tice, Peter	19	Aug. 1865	
Van Horn	27	Dec. 1862	Disability
Walser, Charles	24	Aug. 1862	Disability
Whitmore, Lewis F.	24	July 1863	Killed in action
Wildt, Fred R.	19	Dec. 1862	Killed in action

Name		Age	End of Service	Remarks
Williams, Edwin K.		19	June 1862	Killed in action
Wilson, David A.		20	Sept. 1861	Disability
Wilson, Henry H.		29	Jan. 1862	Disability
Wright, James H.		22	Feb. 1866	
Zimmerman, Dions		24	May 1864	Died of wounds

COMPANY E

Name	Enlistment Rank	Age	End of Service	Remarks
Lumbard, George W.	Captain	31	May 1864	Died of wounds
Doolittle, Charles C.	First Lt.	29	Aug. 1862	Transferred
Parsons, Charles B.	Second Lt.	26	Disability	
Marvin, Charles	First Sgt.	22	Jan. 1863	Hon. Discharged
Emerson, Josiah D.	Sergeant	21	June 1864	
Hewitt, John W.	Sergeant	19	June 1864	
Merritt, Billings B.	Sergeant	23	Oct. 1862	Disability
Theill, William H.	Sergeant	19	Mar. 1863	Court Martial
Abbot, Henry H.	Corporal	22	June 1864	
Brock, David C.	Corporal	19	July 1862	Killed in action
Cortright, Levi J.	Corporal	37	Sept. 1861	Died of wounds
Fletcher, Charles J.	Corporal	23	June 1864	
McCarty, William F.	Corporal	24	Nov. 1864	
Tarsney, James	Corporal	23	May 1864	Killed in action
Williams, Ira	Corporal	21	Dec. 1862	Disability
Miller, Fred	Musician	22	June 1864	
Burke, Eli	Musician	61	Aug. 1861	Disability
Fiester, William T.	Musician	21	Feb. 1866	
Bristol, William T.	Wagoner	25	June 1864	
Abbot, Webster, H.		21	Aug. 1863	Disability
Ainsworth, Riley H.		21	Nov. 1863	Died in prison
Allen, Delzon C.		19	Jan. 1863	Disability
Barker, Augustus K.		18	June 1864	
Best, Benjamin		21	May 1864	Killed in action
Bird, William		21	Nov. 1862	Disability
Birge, William H.		21	June 1864	
Bolles, Seth		24	Feb. 1866	
Brown, Chauncey A.		21	Oct. 1862	Disability
Brown, George B.		19	April 1863	Disability
Burnett, Chauncey V.		21	July 1864	
Burtch, Timothy B.		29	Feb. 1865	
Chase, Isaac		19	Jan. 1862	Disability
Comfort, George		22	Mar. 1862	Disability
Crisler, Joseph		18	June 1864	
Critchfield, Jessie D.		27	April 1862	Disability
Decker, Charles W.		18	Feb. 1866	
Dildine, William H.		21	June 1864	
Dolph, Alfred		21	July 1862	Killed in action
Drake, Charles M.		21	Mar. 1862	Disability
Dugan, John F.		23	June 1864	
Farley, John		22	June 1864	
Fleming, John		18	June 1864	
Forncrook, Frank B.		28	July 1862	Killed in action
Fournia, Peter		32	June 1865	
Fox, David		19	June 1864	

Fuller, William R.	21	May 1865	
Gates, George E.	21	July 1861	Disability
Gilchrist, Archibald	23	Jan. 1863	Disability
Gleason, Alvaro F.	21	July 1861	Disability
Green, Newton	22	Sept. 1861	Disability
Gregory, Thomas	23	Nov. 1861	Disability
Hall, Jeremiah M.	27	Mar. 1862	Deserted
Harroun, James H.	22	Feb. 1866	
Hartson, Hiram L.	21	Sept. 1864	
Hollinger, James H.	22	June 1864	
Huff, Thaddeus	20	June 1864	
Hughes, George W.	26	Mar. 1864	Trans. to Invalid Corps
Hunt, F. Marion	21	June 1864	
Iliff, Elias D.	18	July 1862	Died of wounds
Jennison, Sewell A.	23	Mar. 1863	Died of disease
Lake, Amon C.	21	May 1864	Died of wounds
Luce, Moses A.	22	June 1864	
Magee, Henry W.	20	June 1864	
Mallory, Stephen H.	22	June 1864	
Merrifield, Marc A.	21	Nov. 1862	Disability
Metty, Eli	42	Mar. 1863	Disability
Navarre, Alexander	24	Nov. 1863	Trans. to Invalid Corps
Neal, John D.	18	April 1862	Disability
Prestle, Thomas	24	July 1862	Died of wounds
Quackenbush, James A.	19	May 1865	
Randall, Avery	18	Dec. 1861	Died of disease
Rheyport, Charles H.	25	June 1864	
Rodolph, Jacob	22	Sept. 1864	Died of wounds
Rolfe, Jarvis D.	30	Jan. 1863	Disability
Ross, William H.	21	Oct. 1862	Disability
Russell, Justin	21	June 1862	Disability
Simmons, Watson C.	22	April 1864	Disability
Smith, William H.	21	Mar. 1863	
Spence, James K.	28	June 1864	
Spenser, S.		June 1865	
Stacey, George H.	22	June 1864	
Stanback, Philip	19	June 1864	
Stevens, John W.	37	June 1862	Hospitalized; no further record
Stevens, Joseph W.	19	Dec. 1862	Disability
Stone, Oliver P.	18	Nov. 1862	
Strong, Amos	21	Aug. 1865	
Taylor, Edward M.	18	Feb. 1864	Disability
Taylor, Mark W.	21	June 1864	Disability
Van Volkenburgh, Thomas	23	Feb. 1863	Disability
Waller, Francis	20	June 1864	
Ward, George T.	18	June 1864	
Weaver, Orland F.	21		Disability
Whitmore, John B.	24	June 1862	Deserted
Wier, Archibald	23	June 1864	
Wilber, Albert M.	24	Dec. 1862	Disability
Worden, David	30	April 1862	Died of disease
Worden, William M.	42	Mar. 1863	Died of disease
Wright, Lawrence	18	Nov. 1862	

Name		19	Nov. 1862	Disability

Wright, Walter W.   19   Nov. 1862   Disability

COMPANY F

Name	Enlistment Rank	Age	End of Service	Remarks
De Golyer, Samuel	Captain	33	Jan. 1862	Transferred
Preston, Simon B.	First Lt.	35	June 1862	Died of wounds
Smith, Joseph L.	Second Lt.	31	Mar. 1863	Disability, wounds
Wilcox, Harrison	First Sgt.	21	Sept. 1861	Deserted
Lawson, George C.	Sergeant	27	Aug. 1861	Killed in action
Lenbocker, William	Sergeant	26	Nov. 1863	Died in prison
Miner, Ervin S.	Sergeant	28	Dec. 1863	Trans. to Invalid Corps
Schnickenburger, Jn.	Sergeant	27	May 1864	Missing in action
Terpening, William	Sergeant	21	Oct. 1862	Disability
Ball, Allen	Corporal	27	June 1864	Disability
Brownell, John	Corporal	21	Oct. 1863	Died in prison
Goodsell, George A.	Corporal	25	June 1864	
Johnson, Freeman	Corporal	26	July 1863	Trans. to Invalid Corps
Price, George	Corporal	23	Dec. 1862	
Westfall, Benjamin	Corporal	22	June 1864	
Case, Charles C.	Musician	32	July 1862	Died of disease
Cressey, Noah	Musician	52	July 1862	Disability
Smith, Marvin	Musician	27	Feb. 1866	
Parkhurst, James A.	Wagoner	21	June 1864	
Ackley, John		23	Aug. 1862	Died of wounds
Austin, James		28	Oct. 1861	Disability
Bacon, William J.		19	June 1864	
Balcom, William R.		21	Feb. 1863	Disability
Barnes, Henry A.		19	Aug. 1865	Disability
Bing, John		29	Oct. 1862	Disability
Boag, Andrew		18	June 1864	
Bone, Christian N.		27	June 1864	
Brockaw, Zackius		24	Jan. 1864	Trans. to Invalid Corps
Brockway, George		19	Sept. 1861	Died of disease
Buck, Lyman		21	Oct. 1862	Killed in action
Bullard, George W.		39	Aug. 1861	Disability
Butts, Marshall		19	Feb. 1866	
Calhoun, Charles		26	Sept. 1863	Trans. to Invalid Corps
Clark, Frank		19	June 1864	
Cogswell, John H.		18	Dec. 1861	Deserted
Comstock, Harrison		20	June 1864	
Connor, John		33	Aug. 1861	Deserted
Cotrell, Dion H.		18	Sept. 1862	
Coville, Andrew		24	July 1863	Missing in action
Cronk, David		22	June 1861	Died of disease
Dann, Reuben		22	April 1864	Deserted
Delany, John		21	July 1862	Disability
Dickerson, James B.		34	Aug. 1862	Disability
Dillon, John			Sept. 1864	

Name	Age	Date	Fate
Dillon, William B.	20	Dec. 1863	Died in prison
Fausett, Francis	31	Dec. 1862	Disability
Folwell, William R.	26	Oct. 1862	Disability
Ford, Oscar	23	Aug. 1861	Disability
Fountain, Hiram B.	19	July 1863	Killed in action
Fowler, Hudson K.	21	June 1862	Disability
Freeman, Allen	21	June 1865	
Gue, Leonard L.	26	Mar. 1864	Trans. to Invalid Corps
Haight, Benjamin	32	May 1862	Died of disease
Hamilton, Joseph H.	25	April 1863	Died of wounds
Hammond, Lucius G.	41	Sept. 1863	Trans. to Invalid Corps
Hamp, Frederick	40	May 1862	Disability
Hamp, William	19	June 1863	Deserted
Hassington, Addison J.	19	July 1863	Killed in action
Heath, Charles	18	Mar. 1863	Died of disease
Heath, Chauncy	20	June 1864	
Hilliard, Alfred J.	19	June 1864	
Holister, Alvin F.	22	July 1861	Deserted
Ingall, Henry E.	18	June 1862	
Johnson, Thomas A.	41	Aug. 1861	Disability
Judson, Thomas H.	22	May 1864	Killed in action
Kenyon, Lewis L.	19	July 1862	Killed in action
Lawrence, Henry L.	21	May 1863	Died of wounds
Lewis, George W.	25	Feb. 1864	Trans. to Invalid Corps
Lewis, Harvey	21	June 1865	
Lossing, Jehial B.	18	Jan. 1863	Disability
Miliken, John	18	Nov. 1862	Deserted
Miner, Austin D.	20	May 1863	Killed in action
Mott, Charles	20	July 1862	Died of wounds
Murphy, William W.	19	July 1862	Killed in action
Owen, Martin W.	24	Feb. 1866	
Palmer, William H.	24	June 1864	Killed in action
Parmalee, Noble S.	20	June 1864	
Paskett, George	22	Oct. 1862	Disability
Peters, Charles W.	18	July 1862	Killed in action
Rierson, Henry	24	Nov. 1861	Deserted
Roberts, Russell	22	Aug. 1861	Disability
Russell, Jeremiah	18	Dec. 1862	Disability
Severance, Morris P.	21	Oct. 1862	Disability
Silsbee, George W.	30	Aug. 1862	Disability
Smith, Albert	19	July 1863	Missing in action
Smith, John	19	June 1864	
Smith, Nathaniel M.	21	June 1864	
Stutson, Joseph F.	31	Mar. 1863	Died of disease
Sullinger, Asa	33	Aug. 1861	Disability
Terpening, William H.	31	Aug. 1861	Disability
Tuttle, James G.	21	June 1862	Disability
Van Houten, Thaddeus	24	Jan. 1862	Disability
VanDaveter, William	26	Nov. 1862	Disability
Walker, Hinckley	19	Aug. 1861	Disability
Warner, George P.	20	Aug. 1861	Deserted
Wheeler, Chester G.	28	Aug. 1861	Disability
Wheeler, Edward H.	24	Sept. 1861	Died of disease

Name		Age	End of Service	Remarks
Wilcox, Charles W.		21	Sept. 1861	Deserted
Williams, Edwin W.		18	Feb. 1866	
Wirts, Stiles H.		18	May 1862	
Woodward, Harlow W.		18	June 1861	Disability

COMPANY G

Name	Enlistment Rank	Age	End of Service	Remarks
Marshall, David D.	Captain	34	June 1864	
Montieth, George	First Lt.	21	Jan. 1865	
Beers, Jeptha W.	Second Lt.	40	July 1862	Died of wounds
Allen, Jerome	First Sgt.	32	June 1864	
Allen, Samuel	Sergeant	23	June 1862	Died of wounds
Allison, John M.	Sergeant	19	Dec. 1861	Died of disease
Deuel, Frederick P.	Sergeant	22	Oct. 1862	Disability
Rodgers, John L.	Sergeant	31	Feb. 1863	Hon. discharge
Curtis, Ambrose	Corporal	21	June 1864	
Dickinson, John E.	Corporal	21	June 1864	
Hall, John L.	Corporal		Feb. 1866	
Mangus, James	Corporal	25	Dec. 1862	Died of disease
McKeown, James	Corporal	19	Nov. 1861	Died of disease
Mead, LeRoy	Corporal	30	June 1864	
Shaw, George	Corporal	26		Hospitalized; no further record
Slater, John M.	Corporal	32	Nov. 1861	Disability
Austin, Lorenzo D.	Musician	43	Oct. 1862	Disability
Abrahamskie, Paul		43	Oct. 1862	Disability
Aesenhuth, August		20	Oct. 1863	Disability
Allen, Jesse I.		20	Aug. 1861	Disability
Allen, Tristam C.		28	May 1864	Wounded and Missing
Anderson, James B.		21	Oct. 1862	Disability
Avery, Burgess M.		21	Dec. 1861	Died of disease
Barrett, Charles H.		18	Feb. 1866	
Besinger, Antone		27	Oct. 1862	Disability, wounds
Bissell, Henry		21	June 1864	
Cassidy, James H.		20		Unknown discharge
Clement, Arthur		19	June 1864	
Coleman, Levi B.		28	Feb. 1866	
Conklin, Wesley R.		21	Sept. 1861	
Daniels, Harrison		24	June 1864	
Davis, Wilson		21	Sept. 1861	Died of disease
Dunphey, Anderson W.		20	June 1864	
Fenton, Asahel		23	Oct. 1862	Disability
Fogle, George		19	Dec. 1862	Killed in action
Fullerton, John		18	Dec. 1861	Disability
Gauntlett, Richard		18	June 1864	
Gee, Orrin		22	Jan. 1864	Trans. to Invalid Corps
Gooding, Charles W.		24	Aug. 1861	Disability
Hall, Lorenzo		22	Oct. 1862	Disability
Hampton, Charles		19	June 1864	

Name	Age	Date	Status
Henderson, William	22	June 1864	
Hibiner, Daniel	22	June 1864	
Hoagland, Thomas V.	22	June 1864	
Hough, Judson B.	27	May 1863	Missing in action
Huffman, Samuel	27	May 1863	Missing in action
Irwin, James	22	Dec. 1862	Disability, wounds
Kelly, William H.	34	June 1864	
Larzaleer, William F.	19	Sept. 1861	Disability
Lee, Andrew J.	22	June 1864	
Lindsley, William	21	June 1864	
Mackey, John H.	25	Feb. 1866	
Marcey, Lyman	25	Sept. 1864	
Mather, William	18	Aug. 1861	Died in hospital
Mathews, William	18	Oct. 1861	Deserted
Miner, John	25	July 1862	Died of wounds
Monroe, Calvin	21	July 1862	Killed in action
Monotonye, Sidney B.	22	Feb. 1866	
Morgan, Moses	40	Feb. 1866	Disability
Murry, Charles	19		
North, John W.	23	June 1864	
North, William P.	21	July 1862	Died of wounds
Olmstead, Edwin		Jan. 1866	Disability
Olmstead, Lewis	24	June 1864	
Owen, Andrew	22	June 1864	
O'Brien, Michael	21	June 1864	
Pennock, Martin V.	19	Jan. 1864	Died of disease
Peterson, John	21	Dec. 1861	
Pierson, William C.		June 1862	Killed in action
Plum, Charles	21	May 1864	Killed in action
Plummer, Chester W.	18	May 1863	Killed in action
Plummer, William H.	21	June 1864	
Randel, Albert L.	19	June 1862	Disability
Rankin, Erastus	22	June 1864	
Rankin, Simon	19	May 1863	Missing in action
Rapson, John	22	Feb. 1866	
Richmond, James	21	Mar. 1863	Disability
Rockfellow, Andrew H.	28	July 1864	Killed in action
Sadler, Silas W.	18	June 1864	
Saxton, Charles	20	July 1862	Killed in action
Saxton, James	18	June 1864	
Seward, William H.	18	Dec. 1862	Disability
Smith, Lorenzo	23	May 1864	Died of wounds
Snyder, Andrew C.	18	Jan. 1862	Disability
Spafford, Charles R.	26	Aug. 1861	Disability
Taylor, Levi S.	23	June 1864	
Thompson, H.	19		
Tomlinson, Charles	18	June 1864	Killed in action
Totten, Joseph	18	June 1864	
Tripp, Sylvester S.	25	Nov. 1865	
Underwood, Dexter	18	July 1862	Killed in action
Van Lieu, James J.	43	Oct. 1862	Disability
Walters, Erastus	19	June 1865	
Waring, Joshua	19	April 1862	Died of disease
Webster, Loren	22	May 1864	Killed in action
Westgate, Albert	21	July 1862	Killed in action

Name				Feb. 1866	
Wheeler, Frank			21	Feb. 1866	
Whelan, Edwin M.			21	June 1864	
Wright, Samuel F.			26	Aug. 1861	Disability

COMPANY H

Name	Enlistment Rank	Age	End of Service	Remarks
Funk, Moses A.	Captain	47	Sept. 1861	Hon. discharge
Hadley, Simon B.	First Lt.	35	Dec. 1861	
McConnell, William	Second Lt.	23	Jan. 1862	Resigned
Robinson, William F.	First Sgt.	24	May 1864	Disability, wounds
Jeffers, George W.	Sergeant	22	Sept. 1861	Disability
Lindsey, William	Sergeant	21	May 1862	Disability
Parker, Senter S.	Sergeant	22	Jan. 1865	Resigned
Van Allen, Darwin G.	Sergeant	23	Dec. 1862	Disability
Alden, John A.	Sergeant	21	Nov. 1865	
Anderson, Allen	Corporal	22	Jan. 1862	Disability
Birdsall, Charles	Corporal	39	Aug. 1862	Disability
Blatchley, Truman R.	Corporal	21	July 1862	Killed in action
Dean, John	Corporal	28	Feb. 1866	
Staley, John	Corporal	22	June 1864	
Walker, Samuel G.	Corporal		June 1864	
Willis, A. Sidney	Corporal	18		Transferred
Baker, Albert	Musician	19	Jan. 1862	Disability
Warren, John	Wagoner	40	July 1861	Disability
Alexander, William B.		26	Jan. 1865	
Allen, H. Linden		18	Sept. 1862	Disability
Ashmore, Obed S.		19	June 1865	
Bashyet, James H.		35	July 1862	Missing in action
Beebe, Darwin C.		21	Dec. 1862	Disability
Benett, Alexander C.		25	Oct. 1863	Died in prison
Benett, George H.		19	July 1862	Killed in action
Boyles, John		21	Oct. 1864	
Butland, Benjamin		19	June 1862	Died of wounds
Case, Henry L.		22	June 1865	Disability
Cobb, David T.		21	Jan. 1863	Disability
Coleman, Isaac		34	July 1862	Died of disease
Coleman, John		35	July 1863	Trans. to Invalid Corps
Daniels, Montross		21	July 1861	Transferred
Davis, William		21	April 1863	Disability
Dodge, Alvin		24	Mar. 1864	Disability
Dodge, Hiram		23	June 1864	
Fuller, Watson W.		26	July 1862	Died of wounds
Furman, Edward		25	Dec. 1862	Died of disease
Getter, Origen H.		26	Feb. 1866	
Gilbert, Oliver		24	Oct. 1861	Died of disease
Gregery, Charles W.		18	July 1863	Killed in action
Hadley, Jesse L.		21	Dec. 1861	Disability
Hamp, Clark G.		18	June 1864	
Hardy, John D.		24	June 1864	Missing in action
Harris, Charles W.		18	Feb. 1863	Disability

Name	Age	Date	Reason
Henry, James	25	Jan. 1863	Disability, wounds
Howe, Marion F.	21	Dec. 1861	Disability
Jeffers, Charles T.	24	Dec. 1861	Disability, wounds
Johnson, James H.	20	June 1862	Died of disease
Jones, Miles	18	Mar. 1863	Disability
Kiney, George H.	21	Dec. 1862	Disability, wounds
LaFleur, Asher B.	21	June 1865	
Marks, William H.	21	Feb. 1866	
Marsh, William H.	19	Sept. 1865	
McConnell, Martin	21	Aug. 1862	Died of disease
McKiver, Robert	18	May 1862	Disability
Miller, Michael	19	Nov. 1861	Disability
Millions, John	22	July 1862	Killed in action
Morehouse, Henry L.	19	July 1862	Killed in action
Morehouse, William M.	19	Jan. 1863	Disabililty
Mosher, Abraham	27	July 1862	Disability
Mosher, Nathaniel	21	Feb. 1866	
Murdock, Ira	24	July 1861	Disability
Nash, Orlando	19	Jan. 1861	Disability
Nobles, Enos S.	21	Feb. 1866	
Nulton, Byron F.	21	Nov. 1861	Disability
Ostrander, James H.	19	Sept. 1861	Disability
Page, Erastus W.	18	Jan. 1862	Disability
Parker, Horatio B.	21	Aug. 1862	Died of disease
Parker, Samuel S.	41	Jan. 1862	Disability
Parks, Orson L.	28	Nov. 1862	Disability
Pendelton, James H.	18	July 1863	Killed in action
Pitwood, John	18	July 1861	Disability
Ranch, Peter	36	Jan. 1863	Disability
Robinson, William W.	21	July 1865	Transferred
Sandbar, Joseph		Feb. 1866	
Scholfield, Lester T.	22	Nov. 1862	Disability
Sloan, William H.	22	Dec. 1861	Died of disease
Smith, Hubert D.	23	June 1864	
Smith, Jarvis		Sept. 1862	Deserted
Smith, Olney J.	19	Nov. 1862	Disability
Smith, William	19	Jan. 1863	Disability
Spade, Abraham	21	July 1862	Killed in action
Stilwel, James I.	19	Jan. 1865	
Taylor, Samuel	24	April 1862	Died of wounds
Ten Eyck, Morley S.	18	Sept. 1861	Disability
Todd, Elan J.	18	Sept. 1862	Died of disease
Tripp, Edwin G.	19	July 1863	Died of wounds
Upthegrove, Henry	18	Jan. 1862	Disability
Vanderpool, Oliver C.	18	July 1862	Killed in action
VanMeeter, Madison	21	Aug. 1861	Died of disease
VanScotter, Alonzo B.	30	Dec. 1862	Disability, wounds
White, Charles P.	22	Nov. 1861	Disability
Wilder, William	22	July 1861	Disability
Williams, Jules L.	20	Jan. 1862	Disability
Wilson, Charles	19	July 1863	Died of wounds
Woods, James T.	25	Aug. 1862	Died of disease

Name		Age	Service	Remarks
Yauger, Francis		20	May 1862	Died of disease
Yawger, Chester S.		19	Jan. 1865	
Young, Lafayette		18	Sept. 1862	Disability, wounds

COMPANY I

Name	Enlisment Rank	Age	Service	End of Remarks
Slocum, Jeremiah D.	Captain	24	Sept. 1862	Hon. discharge
Granger, David A.	Captain	33	June 1861	Transferred
Chapin, Marshall W.	First Lt.	30	Sept. 1862	Transferred
Heintzen, George	First Sgt.	30	July 1862	
Bancroft, John M.	Sergeant	18	June 1864	
Hills, John	Sergeant	23	June 1864	
Vreeland, Michael J.	Sergeant	22	May 1866	
Cooper, John F.	Corporal	27	June 1864	
Couse, Edward G.	Corporal	19		Transferred
Goodell, Titus	Corporal	19	Jan. 1865	Transferred
Maltz, George L.	Corporal	19	June 1864	
Martin, James	Corporal	26	Dec. 1861	Transferred
McDonald, Charles	Corporal	31	Mar. 1863	Disability
Plummer, James	Corporal	31	May 1863	Transferred
Seage, R. Watson	Corporal	23	Dec. 1863	Disability, wounds
Gordon, John A.	Corporal		June 1864	
Leming, Henry A.	Musician	14	Mar. 1863	Disability
Scully, Andrew	Musician	17	Jan. 1863	Disability
Jones, Abiathar H.	Wagoner	30	June 1864	
Alban, William K.		20	July 1861	Deserted
Allen, William H.		21	Feb. 1865	
Bailey, Thomas		45	Sept. 1863	Trans. to Invalid Corps
Bates, Ezra		24	June 1862	Missing in action
Breen, William P.		19	Jan. 1864	Trans. to Invalid Corps
Bronson, William H.		20	July 1862	Killed in action
Burrow, Charles		23	Jan. 1863	Trans. to Invalid Corps
Burwell, Peter Jr.		18		Disability
Campau, Claude		19	April 1864	Discharged
Carpenter, Philip		19	June 1864	Died of wounds
Carson, Darius H.		25	June 1864	
Clago, James E.		23	June 1862	Killed in action
Clarke, Horace A.		20	July 1862	Killed in action
Clarke, Joseph D.		18	April 1863	Disability
Craig, Orlando		21	Dec. 1862	Died of wounds
Cramer, Richard L.		18	Feb. 1863	Disability
Cross, Lorenzo		34	June 1861	Deserted
Cunningham, Henry		19	Nov. 1862	Disability
Davis, James		19	Feb. 1866	
Diehl, Aaron J.		25	Nov. 1862	Disability
Doyle, Cornelius		19	Sept. 1863	Trans. to Invalid Corps
Eastman, Norris		18	Dec. 1862	

Name	Age	Date	Cause
Eliot, Elmer	30	June 1864	
Enos, Lewis N.	20	April 1865	Died of wounds
Fenton, James	39	May 1864	Died of wounds
Fitzpatrick, John	23	June 1862	Missing in action
Forbes, Andrew		June 1862	Missing in action
Goodell, Thomas	21	Feb. 1866	
Haight, Daniel M.	24	June 1864	
Haven, William W.	19	July 1862	Died of wounds
Hogan, Thomas	32	June 1862	Killed in action
Hollingstead, James B.	22	July 1862	Killed in action
Hoy, Hugh	19	Feb. 1866	
Hubbell, Jerome	23	Oct. 1862	Disability
Hyndell, John	20	April 1863	Disability
Jackson, William H.	20	July 1863	Killed in action
Jehu, David	41	Aug. 1863	Accidental death
Kesselring, Jacob	22	Nov. 1862	Disability
Keyes, William	38	Dec. 1861	Disability
Kruger, Christian	22	June 1864	
Kydd, John H.	19	July 1863	Killed in action
LaFountain, Paul	25	Oct. 1861	Died of disease
Lapham, George	19	July 1863	Killed in action
Lapham, William B.	22	Feb. 1862	Disability
Leighton, Philip	23	Dec. 1862	Killed in action
Loss, Charles P.	18	June 1864	
Lovett, George	21	June 1864	
Martin, Richard	18	Jan. 1862	Disability
McCann, James	23	June 1864	
McClurg, William R.	24	Aug. 1861	Disability
McDonald, Robert S.	22	Oct. 1862	Disability
McEvoy, John	21	June 1864	
McFarland, John	19	June 1864	
McKnight, George	27	Sept. 1861	Suicide
Miller, John M.	23	July 1862	Died of wounds
Mooney, John	22	July 1861	Deserted
Mott, Sylvanus Jr.	19	July 1862	Died of disease
Nichols, James	23	June 1864	
Potterfield, Samuel D.	22	July 1862	Died of wounds
Regets, John	24	June 1864	
Reneau, Peter	21	Jan. 1863	Disability
Robinson, William G.	21	Sept. 1862	Disability
Romeyn, James W.		Oct. 1862	Resigned
Rumsey, Reuben W.	23	Aug. 1861	Died of disease
Saliotte, Gilbert	19	June 1864	
Schutze, Charles L.	25	July 1862	Killed in action
Smith, George	21	July 1861	Disability
Springer, Arnold D.	18	Aug. 1863	Trans. to Invalid Corps
Stevenson, Isaiah	27	Aug. 1863	Trans. to Invalid Corps
Stoddard, Nolton F.	27	Nov. 1862	Hon. discharge
Stoddard, William H.	22	Aug. 1863	Disability
Stott, Mark	30	June 1864	
Stout, William	20	May 1863	Missing in action
Trombly, Richard	23	June 1861	Disability
Twing, Edwin	31	Oct. 1861	Died of disease
Vreeland, William J.	19	July 1861	Disability

Name		Age		Remarks
Wait, Alonzo		19	Jan. 1863	Disability, wounds
Weatherwax, Charles		21	Oct. 1862	
Weeks, Robert		27	Nov. 1863	
Wheeler, John		21	Oct. 1862	Disability, wounds
Wilkinson, John		43	April 1863	Disability
Wisdom, Albert		19	May 1863	
Woods, William		44	April 1862	Disability
Young, George A.		27	April 1864	Died on furlough
Youngs, Henry L.		18	July 1861	Disability

COMPANY K

Name	Enlistment Rank	Age	End of Service	Remarks
Crane, Alexander D.	Captain	44	July 1861	Disability
Jeffords, Harrison H.	First Lt.	24	July 1863	Died of wounds
Mulloy, James	Second Lt.	40	July 1861	Hon. discharge
Iling, William G.	First Sgt.		June 1862	Killed in action
Bailey, Isreal	Sergeant	45	Nov. 1861	Disability
Bush, Ransom	Sergeant	37	Sept. 1862	Died of disease
McLean, James R.	Sergeant	28	April 1864	Disability
Sharp, Jonathan S.	Sergeant	27	May 1864	
Conkey, James R.	Corporal	35	July 1865	Disability
Easton, Ambrose L.	Corporal	30	June 1862	Killed in action
Hawks, James E.	Corporal	23	April 1864	Died of disease
Noble, Edgar	Corporal	22	Aug. 1865	Disability
Potter, Alvinza	Corporal	25	Sept. 1863	Trans. to Invalid Corps
Smith, Julius D.	Corporal	21	July 1861	Disability
Wilcox, Calvin	Corporal	21	Sept. 1861	Disability
Bailey, William H.	Musician	21	Jan. 1866	
Savery, Stephen P.	Musician	20	July 1861	Disability
Crane, Martin L.	Wagoner	44	Aug. 1861	Disability
Abbott, James G.		21	June 1862	Died of disease
Austin, Albert		20	Oct. 1862	Transferred
Baker, Moses W.		21	June 1864	
Barlow, Charles H.		21	Feb. 1863	Unknown discharge
Barnes, Joel H.			1865	Disability, wounds
Baryan, Lorenzo		20	Mar. 1862	Disability
Bennett, William		20	Oct. 1862	Transferred
Billson, Henry		24	Dec. 1862	Died of disease
Blankman, George		20		Missing in action
Blodgett, Worster		27	Nov. 1862	Disability, wounds
Boothby, Henry		23	Dec. 1861	Disability
Bostwick, Charles		24	Mar. 1862	Deserted
Boucher, Charles W.		24	Nov. 1861	Disability
Brown, Ezra		22	June 1864	
Browner, Eugene		18	Oct. 1862	Transferred
Carpenter, Eastman G.		21	Feb. 1866	
Collins, John		21	July 1861	Deserted

Cook, Harrison P.	20	July 1862	Disability
Crane, Alexander B.	23	Sept. 1862	Disability, wounds
Crane, George	24	Nov. 1861	Disability
Cranston, William		June 1865	Deserted
Croghan, George		Oct. 1862	
Cunningham, William J.	22	May 1864	Killed in action
Demming, Benjamin O.	18	Jan. 1862	Disability
Donley, Giles G.	21	Jan. 1864	Trans. to Invalid Corps
Dorn, John J.	22	May 1862	Died of disease
Downer, Jacob R.	23	Dec. 1861	Disability
Drew, William H.	23	Aug. 1865	
Field, William H.	18	June 1864	
Fishbeck, Stephen G.	21	Sept. 1862	Deserted
Foster, Martin L.	23	Aug. 1865	
Garrison, Samuel J.	32	Aug. 1861	Disability
Gould, William H.	21	June 1864	
Griswold, Lewis C.	18	Oct. 1862	Transferred
Harris, Henry H.	22	June 1864	
Haviland, Delos M.	20	June 1862	Killed in action
Haviland, Lewes A.	24	Jan. 1863	Disability, wounds
Hodge, Riley	22	Oct. 1862	Transferred
Hodges, Theodore	18	Dec. 1861	Died of disease
Hoffman, Felix		Mar. 1863	Disability, wounds
Holt, Ira E.	21	Mar. 1863	Disability, wounds
House, Eri	31	Aug. 1862	Disability, wounds
Hyatt, James E.	27	June 1864	
Ide, Brainard T.	21	Aug. 1861	Died of disease
Jewett, George	19	June 1861	Deserted
Kane, Morris	35	Sept. 1863	Trans. to Invalid Corps
Kelley, Robert W.	18	Dec. 1862	Disability, wounds
Kellogg, E. Lyman	19	June 1864	
Kelsh, Henry	43	Sept. 1861	Disability, wounds
Lampman, Amasa	24	Dec. 1861	Disability
Lampman, Lawson W.	18	July 1863	Killed in action
Laughlin, Patrick	20	Oct. 1862	Transferred
Mann, Harlow S.	20	June 1862	Disability
Martin, Culwell		Sept. 1862	Disability
McCaussey, Charles	21	April 1863	Disability, wounds
Moodie, Robert	22	July 1863	Died of wounds
Murphy, Edward H.	21	June 1861	Died of disease
O'Neill, John	30	June 1864	
Percy, Perrin E.			
Perkins, Guy C.	18	Jan. 1863	Disability
Perkins, Leonard W.	39	Feb. 1863	Disability
Perry, Orrin E.	31	Feb. 1865	
Petre, Henry	19	June 1864	

147

Name	Age	Date	Notes
Poyer, Daniel F.	21	May 1864	Killed in action
Riley, Luke	21	Oct. 1862	Transferred
Roney, Barney	22	July 1862	Killed in action
Sawyer, Charles E.	19	June 1864	
Sherry, Thomas	18	June 1864	
Smith, Austin T.	21	Feb. 1863	Died of disease
Smith, George W.	18	Aug. 1861	Disability
Smith, Herman	19	Feb. 1866	
Smith, William H.	20	July 1864	Transferred
Storms, Abram W.		Aug. 1865	
Torpy, Silvanus E.	27	Sept. 1862	Disability
Tucker, John M.	21	Aug. 1862	Disability, wounds
Tuffs, John	18	Oct. 1862	Transferred
Tuffs, Richard M.	21	Oct. 1862	Transferred
Tuttle, Moses L.	25	July 1862	Disability
Tuttle, Smith	25		
VanDeMark, Abram	20	Nov. 1862	Disability
Vanzile, Riley E.	21	June 1863	Missing on march
Vanzile, Wells	22	July 1863	Trans. to Invalid Corps
Walterhouse, Daniel L.	32	July 1863	
Wheelock, John F.	30	June 1864	
Wilsay, Solomon	32	July 1862	Disability
Yearnce, William H.	21	June 1861	

Appendix Three
List of Engagements
May 24, 1862, through June 18, 1864

Battle	State	Date
New Bridge	Virginia	May 24, 1862
Hanover Court House	Virginia	May 27, 1862
Mechanicsville	Virginia	June 26, 1862
Gaines' Mill	Virginia	June 27, 1862
Savage Station	Virginia	June 29, 1862
Turkey Bend	Virginia	June 30, 1862
White Oak Swamp	Virginia	June 30, 1862
Malvern Hill	Virginia	July 1, 1862
Harrison's Landing	Virginia	July 2, 1862
Gainesville	Virginia	August 29, 1862
Second Bull Run	Virginia	August 30, 1862
Antietam	Maryland	Sept. 17, 1862
Sheperdstown Ford	Virginia	Sept. 20, 1862
Snicker's Gap	Virginia	Nov. 14, 1862
Fredericksburg	Virginia	Dec. 13, 1862
Morrisville	Virginia	Dec. 30, 1862
U.S. Ford	Virginia	January 1, 1863
Chancellorsville	Virginia	May 1-5, 1863
Kelly's Ford	Virginia	June 9, 1863
Ashby's Gap	Virginia	June 21, 1863
Gettysburg	Pennsylvania	July 1-3, 1863
Williamsport	Maryland	July 12, 1863
Wapping Heights	Virginia	July 21, 1863
Culpepper	Virginia	Oct. 13, 1863
Brandy Station	Virginia	Oct. 13, 1863
Bristoe Station	Virginia	Oct. 14, 1863
Rappahannock Station	Virginia	Nov. 28, 1863
Cross-Roads	Virginia	Nov. 28, 1863
Mine Run	Virginia	Nov. 29, 1863

Wilderness	Virginia	May 5-7, 1864
Laurel Hill	Virginia	May 8, 1864
Po River	Virginia	May 10, 1864
Spotsylvania	Virginia	May 12, 1864
Ny River	Virginia	May 21, 1864
North Anna	Virginia	May 23, 1864
Jericho Mills	Virginia	May 24, 1864
Noel's Turn	Virginia	May 26, 1864
Totopotomy	Virginia	May 30, 1864
Magnolia Swamp	Virginia	June 1, 1864
Bethesda Church	Virginia	June 2, 1864
Petersburg	Virginia	June 18, 1864

Appendix Four
Initial Companies at Unit Muster, June 20, 1861, Adrian, Michigan

Company A
Smith Guards of Monroe, Michigan
Capt. Constant Luce
First Lt. John M. Oliver
Second Lt. A. Morrell Rose

Company B
Adrian Volunteers of Adrian, Michigan
Capt. James H. Cole
First Lt. Jeremiah D. Slocum
Second Lt. James E. Avery

Company C
Peninsular Guard of Sturgis, Michigan
Capt. Abram R. Wood
First Lt. Henry A. Grannis
Second Lt. Ebenezer French

Company D
Barry Guard of Ann Arbor, Michigan
Capt. John M. Randolph
First Lt. Richard G. DePuy
Second Lt. Jaruis W. Hall

Company E
Hillsdale Volunteers of Hillsdale, Michigan
Capt. George W. Lumbard
First Lt. Charles C. Doolittle
Second Lt. Charles B. Parsons

Company F

Hudson Volunteers of Hudson, Michigan
Capt. Samuel DeGolyer
First Lt. Simon B. Preston
Second Lt. Joseph L. Smith

Company G
Tecumseh Volunteers of Tecumseh, Michigan
Capt. David D. Marshall
First Lt. George Montieth
Second Lt. Jeptha W. Beers

Company H
Grosvenor Union Guard of Jonesville, Michigan
Capt. Moses A. Funk
First Lt. Simon B. Hadley
Second Lt. William H. McConnell

Company I
Trenton Volunteers of Trenton, Michigan
Capt. David A. Granger
First Lt. Marshall W. Chapin
Second Lt. Francis S. Earle

Company K
Dexter Union Guard of Dexter, Michigan
Capt. Alexander D. Crane
First Lt. Harrison H. Jeffords
Second Lt. James Mulloy

Appendix Five
Burial Sites of 4th Michigan Veterans

The soldiers whose graves appear herein all received care and final burial at the Grand Rapids Home For Veterans located in Grand Rapids, Michigan. The home was built in 1886 specifically for the care of Civil War soldiers and their widows. The cemetery was laid out in the shape of a Maltese Cross with a large statue at its center. Although the cemetery has expanded, the shape of the Maltese Cross can still be discerned as the initial five burial sections are bordered by both paved and sunken dirt roads. The cemetery contains the remains of over thirty-five veterans of the 4th Michigan and Reorganized 4th Michigan Infantry. Burial sites located in other Michigan communities are also included in this appendix.

photograph by Ken Oberholtzer

Michigan Soldiers' Home

As you enter the secured cemetery of the Michigan Soldiers' Home, now known as the Grand Rapids Home For Veterans, one immediately notices the peacefulness and tranquillity of the setting. Before you is a historical marker that describes the cemetery and its layout. Behind and to both sides are rather large duck ponds that feed a fast flowing stream emptying into the Grand River a quarter mile away. Before you and on both sides is the rising ground of the cemetery now shaded by large, fully grown oak trees. To the immediate right and forward is a set of three flag poles with a dedication and re-dedication plaque.

photograph by Ken Oberholtzer

Cemetery Monument

Proceeding up the road, past the three flag poles on the right and through the towering oaks you pass a sunken road on your left which is one of the original boundaries of the Maltese Cross layout. Continuing on you encounter the central monument to all the Civil War veterans. It is in the center of the Maltese Cross and from this location the outer most boundaries of the Maltese Cross can be seen. The soldier faces the first section of the original cemetery, to his right is the second oldest section, to his left is the third. The cemetery layout has been converted to a numeric section/row/plot configuration from its original A/B/C designations.

photograph by Ken Oberholtzer

William H. Allen

William Allen, from Lenawee County, enlisted in Company I at the age of twenty-one on June 20, 1861. He was taken prisoner in the Wheatfield and eventually released on November 20, 1864. He returned to active duty and was mustered out in Detroit on February 3, 1865, with the rank of corporal. Allen died of a brain hemorrhage on June 4, 1927. He is buried at the Grand Rapids Home For Veterans, plot 8, row 1, grave 7.

photograph by Ken Oberholtzer

Henry A. Barnes

Henry Barnes, of Lenawee County, enlisted in Company F at the age of nineteen on June 20, 1861. He was wounded on May 5, 1864, during the Wilderness battle, and again at Hatchers Run on February 6, 1865. He was later discharged for disability in Philadelphia on August 26, 1865. Barnes died of heart disease on February 2, 1917. He is buried at the Grand Rapids Home For Veterans, plot 6, row 11, grave 10.

photograph by Ken Oberholtzer

Jackson Charter

Jackson Charter, from Monroe County, enlisted in Company A at the age of twenty-two on June 20, 1861. He was unharmed at Gettysburg but was later wounded at the Wilderness on May 5, 1864. Charter remained in active duty until the end of his enlistment. He was mustered out on June 30, 1864, in Detroit. Charter died of epilepsy on July 7, 1907. He is buried at the Grand Rapids Home For Veterans, plot 4, row 14, grave 44.

photograph by Ken Oberholtzer

Elvi Cicott

Elvi Cicott enlisted in Company A on June 20, 1861, at the age of thirty-five. Corporal Cicott received a disability discharge in Monroe, Michigan, on August 1, 1863; whether this discharge was related to the injury he sustained at the Wheatfield is undetermined. It is known, however, that Cicott was hospitalized until February 20, 1863, at the general hospital on Davids Island, New York, for "disease of the bladder." He died on September 15, 1908. He is buried at the Grand Rapids Home For Veterans, plot 5, row 1, grave 4.

photograph by Ken Oberholtzer

Giles Donley

Giles Donley, of Livingston County, enlisted in Company K on June 20, 1861. He was transferred to the Invalid Corps on January 15, 1864. Donley died of heart disease on September 16, 1906. He is buried at the Grand Rapids Home For Veterans, plot 4, row 20, grave 9.

photograph by Ken Oberholtzer
Henry A. Leming

Young Henry Leming, from Wayne County, enlisted in Company I at the age of fourteen on June 20, 1861, as a musician. He received a disability discharge just 104 days before the Wheatfield, on March 16, 1863. Leming died of heart failure on June 2, 1901. He is buried at the Grand Rapids Home For Veterans, plot 4, row 11, grave 6.

photograph by Ken Oberholtzer

George E. Lovett

George Lovett traveled from Calhoun County to Adrian to enlist in Company I on June 20, 1861, at the age of twenty-one. He was unharmed at Gettysburg and remained in active duty until his discharge on June 30, 1864, in Detroit. Lovett died on February 2, 1916. He is buried at the Grand Rapids Home For Veterans, plot 7, row 6, grave 35.

photograph by Ken Oberholtzer

Michael McDonough

Michael McDonough arrived in Adrian from Saugatuck, located along the shores of Lake Michigan, and enlisted in Company C on June 20, 1861, at the age of twenty-one. Corporal McDonough was wounded at Fredericksburg on December 12, 1862. He was transferred to the Invalid Corps at Washington on October 1, 1863. Whether the transfer is related to an injury sustained at the Wheatfield is undetermined. McDonough died of heart disease on June 6, 1898. He is buried at the Grand Rapids Home For Veterans, plot 2, row 10, grave 1.

photograph by Ken Oberholtzer

James H. Murphy

James Murphy, from Washtenaw County, enlisted in Company D at the age of twenty-two on June 20, 1861. Murphy was unharmed at Gettysburg and re-enlisted on December 29, 1863, in Ann Arbor, Michigan. He was mustered out of the Reorganized 4th on February 23, 1866, in San Antonio, Texas. Murphy died on September 28, 1889, of heart disease. He is buried at the Grand Rapids Home For Veterans, plot 3, row 7, grave 10.

photograph by Ken Oberholtzer

Edwin S. Perry

Edwin Perry, from Washtenaw County, enlisted in Company D at the age of twenty-seven on June 20, 1861. He was unharmed at the Wheatfield, and was mustered out of the Reorganized 4th on February 23, 1866, in San Antonio, Texas, with the rank of corporal. Perry died on March 28, 1916. He is buried at the Grand Rapids Home For Veterans, plot 7, row 8, grave 4.

photograph by Ken Oberholtzer

Edwin W. Williams

Edwin Williams, of Lenawee County, enlisted in Company F on June 20, 1861, at the age of eighteen. Williams was unharmed at Gettysburg and reenlisted on February 21, 1864. He was wounded on May 5, 1864, during the Wilderness battle. Williams was mustered out of the Reorganized 4th on February 15, 1866, in San Antonio, Texas. He died on June 12, 1917, of chronic nephritis. He is buried at the Grand Rapids Home For Veterans, plot 7, row 9, grave 21.

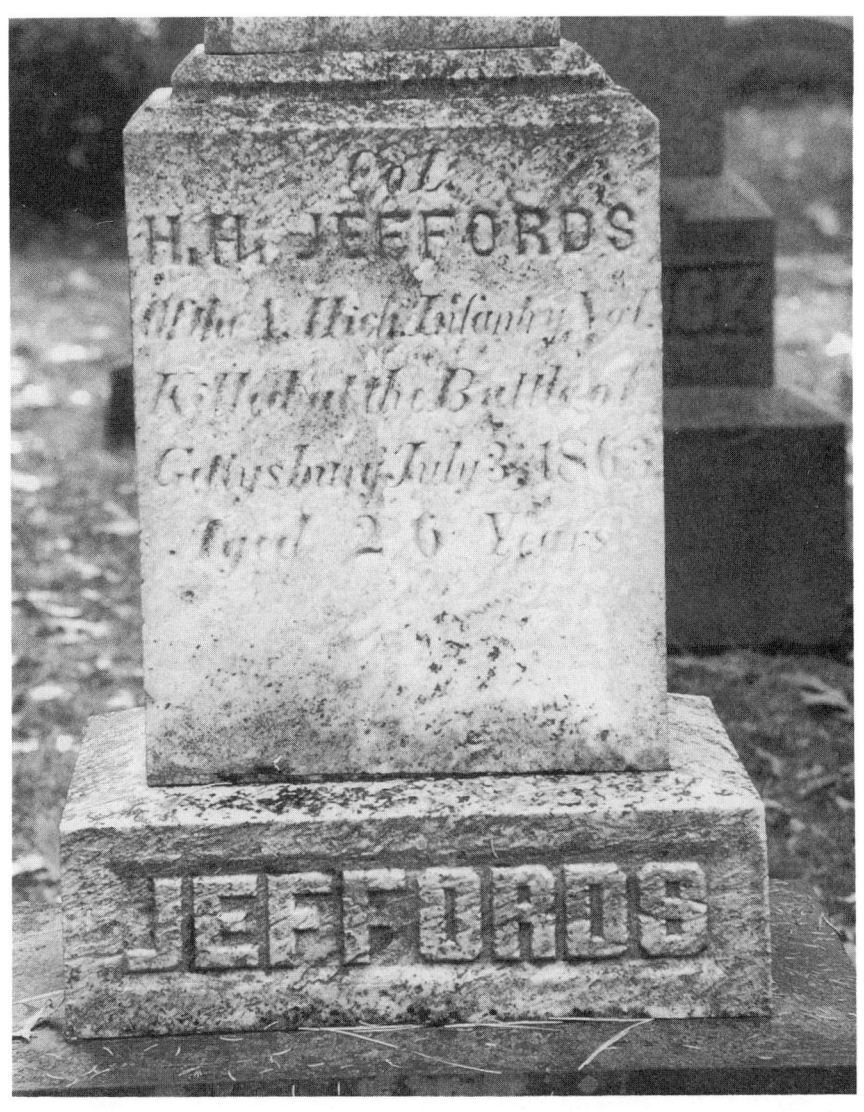

photograph by Ken Oberholtzer

Col. Harrison H. Jeffords

Colonel Jeffords, of Dexter, Michigan, enlisted in Company K in Adrian on June 20, 1861, at the age of twenty-four. Colonel Jeffords valiantly lead the men of the 4th into the Wheatfield but did not survive the onslaught of the Confederates. His body was returned to Dexter, Michigan, and buried in Dexter Cemetery under a nondescript headstone. The pyramidal headstone was placed later, using funds raised by the city of Dexter. The headstone soars into the branches of the towering and shading pine tree.

photograph by Ken Oberholtzer

Richard W. Tuffs

Richard Tuffs, of Washtenaw County, enlisted in Company K in Adrian on June 20, 1861, at the age of twenty-one. He transferred to Battery D of the 5th U.S. Artillery on October 9, 1862, and remained in their service until being discharged in Sharpsburg, Maryland, on October 25, 1862. His younger brother, John, who was eighteen, followed Richard's lead precisely. Richard Tuffs is buried in Dexter Cemetery.

photograph by Ken Oberholtzer

Alexander D. Crane

Alexander Crane, of Washtenaw County, enlisted as captain of Company K in Adrian on June 20, 1861, at the age of forty-four. He was discharged on account of wounds received on July 26, 1861. He is buried in Dexter Cemetery.

photograph by Ken Oberholtzer

William B. Alexander

William Alexander came from Fulton County, Ohio, to enlist in Company H at Adrian on June 20, 1861, at the age of twenty-six. He was wounded in the right hand on September 3, 1862, and was later taken prisoner on the march to Orange Court House, Virginia, on November 27, 1863, and was subsequently sent to Andersonville prison. Alexander was discharged in Detroit on January 31, 1865. He died of heart disease on March 19, 1913. He is buried in Kent City Cemetery, forty miles north of Grand Rapids.

photograph by Ken Oberholtzer

Abram R. Wood

Abram Wood enlisted in Sturgis, Michigan, as captain of Company C at the age of thirty-four. Commissioned on May 16, 1861, he became the first officer of the 4th Michigan to become a casualty of war; he received a mortal wound while on picket duty at Yorktown during McClellan's Peninsular Campaign. He is buried in Sturgis Cemetery.

photograph by Ken Oberholtzer

James Pearsons

James Pearsons, of St. Joseph County, enlisted in Company C on June 20, 1861, at the age of twenty-two. Corporal Pearsons was discharged on disability at Sharpsburg, Maryland, on October 22, 1862. He is buried in Sturgis Cemetery.

photograph by Ken Oberholtzer

Francis M. Skirvin

Francis Skirvin enlisted in Company C on June 20, 1861, at the age of eighteen. He was mustered out on June 30, 1864. He died in 1896 at the age of fifty-three. He is buried in Sturgis Cemetery.

Bibliography

PUBLISHED SOURCES

American Civil War Union Flags. London, England: Osprey Publishing, 1993.

American Civil War Union Uniforms. London, England: Osprey Publishing, 1993.

Barrett, Orvey S. *The Old 4th Michigan Infantry*. Detroit, Michigan: W. S. Ostler, 1888.

Bigelow, John. *The Peach Orchard: Gettysburg, July 2, 1863*. Gettysburg, Pennsylvania: Olde Soldier, 1987.

Bloom, Robert L. *We Never Expected A Battle: The Civilians At Gettysburg*. Gettysburg, Pennsylvania: Adams County Historical Society, 1988.

Brown, G. H. *Record Fourth Michigan Infantry, Civil War 1861 to 1865*. Detroit: Detroit Press Reprint, n.d. Reprint. N.p.: National Historical Society, 1980.

Busey, John W. and David Martin. *Regimental Strengths At Gettysburg*; Baltimore: Gateway Press, 1982.

Campbell, Robert. "Pioneer Memories of the War Days, 1861-1865." In *Historical Collections: Collections and Researches Made by the Michigan Pioneer and Historical Society*. Vol. 30. Lansing, Michigan: Wyncop, Hallenbeck Crawford Co., 1906. 567-72.

Catton, Bruce. *Gettysburg: The Final Fury*. New York: Doubleday, 1974.

Coco, Gregory. *Killed In Action*. Gettysburg, Pennsylvania: Thomas, 1992.

---. *Wasted Valor: The Confederate Dead at Gettysburg*. Gettysburg, Pennsylvania: Thomas, 1990.

---. *A Vast Sea Of Misery*. Gettysburg, Pennsylvania: Thomas, 1988.

Coddington, Edwin B. *The Gettysburg Campaign: A Study in Command*. New York: Scribner, 1968. Reprint. Dayton, Ohio: Morningside, 1979.

Commager, Henry Steel. *The Civil War Almanac*. Lincoln, Nebraska: Bison, 1983.

Coggins, Jack. *Arms And Equipment of The Civil War*. New York: Doubleday, 1962.

Cooling, Benjamin F. and Walton H. Owen. *Mr. Lincoln's Forts*. Shippensburg, Pennsylvania: White Mane, 1988.

Downey, Fairfax. *The Guns At Gettysburg*. New York: McKay, 1959. Reprint. Gaithersburg, Maryland: Olde Soldier, 1987.

Dyer, Frederick C. *Compendium to the War of the Rebellion*. Des Moines, Iowa: Dyer, 1908. Reprint. Dayton, Ohio: Morningside, 1978.

Ellis, Helen. *A Guide To The Material In Detroit Newspapers*. Lansing, Michigan: Publication Commission, 1965.

Faust, Patricia. *Historical Times Illustrated Encyclopedia of the Civil War*. New York: Harper, 1986.

Fox, Frederick. *Regimental Losses in the American Civil War*. New York: Albany, 1889. Reprint. Dayton, Ohio: Morningside, 1985.

Frassanito, William A. *Gettysburg: A Journey In Time*. New York: Scribner, 1975.

Gorden, James. *Arming Michigan's Regiments, 1862-1864*. N.p.: James Genco, 1982.

Hoke, Jacob. *The Great Invasion of 1863*. Dayton, Ohio: Shuey, 1887. Reprint. New York: Yoseloff, 1959.

Hunt, Henry. *Three Days At Gettysburg*. Golden, Colorado: Outbooks, 1981.

Johnson, Robert U. and Clarence Buel, eds. *Battles and Leaders of the Civil War*. 4 vols. New York: Century, 1884-87. Reprint. Secaucus, New Jersey: Castle, 1982.

Johnson, Swafford. *Great Battles Of The Civil War*. Lincoln, Nebraska: Bison, 1984.

Krick, Robert. *Stonewall Jackson At Cedar Mountain*. Chapel Hill: University of North Carolina Press, 1990.

Ladd, David L. and Audrey J. *The Bachelder Papers: Gettysburg in Their Own Words*. 3 vols. Dayton, Ohio: Morningside, 1994-1995.

Luvaas, Jay and Harold W. Nelson, eds. *The U.S. Army War College Guide to the Battle of Gettysburg*. Carlisle, Pennsylvania: South Mountain, 1986.

Magner, Blake and Mike Cavanaugh. *Gettysburg Battle Commanders Photographic Guide*. Collingswood, New Jersey: Thomas, 1987.

McNeily, J. S. *Barksdale's Mississippi Brigade At Gettysburg*. Gaithersburg, Maryland: Olde Soldier, 1987.

Miller, Francis Trevelyan. *The Photographic History Of The Civil War*. Vol. 1. New York: Castle, 1957. Reprint. Secaucus, New Jersey: Blue & Grey, 1987.

Nesbitt, John W. *Rebel Rivers.* Mechanicsburg, Pennsylvania: Stackpole, 1993.

Norton, Oliver Willcox. *The Attack And Defense Of Little Round Top.* Dayton, Ohio: Morningside, 1978.

Parker, Francis J. *The Story of the Thirty-Second Massachusetts Infantry.* Boston: Calkins, 1880.

Pfanz, Harry W. *Gettysburg, The Second Day.* Chapel Hill: University of North Carolina Press, 1987.

Powell, Robert. *Recollections Of A Texas Colonel At Gettysburg.* Philadelphia: Weekly Times, n.d. Reprint. Gettysburg, Pennsylvania: Thomas, 1990.

Powell, William Henry. *The Fifth Army Corps.* New York: Putnam, 1896. Reprint. Dayton, Ohio: Morningside, 1984.

Robertson, John, ed. *Michigan In The War.* Lansing, Michigan: George, 1882.

Schildt, John W. *Roads From Gettysburg.* Parsons, West Virginia: McClain, 1979.

---. *Roads to Gettysburg.* Parsons, West Virginia: McClain, 1978.

Seage, Henry. *History Of Company E, 4th Michigan Infantry.* Lansing, Michigan: Thompson & Van Buren, 1897.

Stackpole, Edward J. *Chancellorsville.* Harrisburg, Pennsylvania: Stackpole, 1988.

---. *They Met At Gettysburg.* Harrisburg: Eagle, 1956. Reprint. New York: Bonanza, 1956.

Thomas, Dean. *Ready... Aim... Fire! Small Arms Ammunition At Gettysburg.* Arendtsville, Pennsylvania: Osborn, 1981.

Tucker, Glenn. *High Tide at Gettysburg.* Dayton, Ohio: Morningside, 1983.

United States Department of War. *The War of the Rebellion: A Compilation of the Official Records of the Union and Confederate Armies.* 70 volumes in 128 parts. Washington, D.C.: Government Printing Office, 1880-1901.

Vanderslice, John M. *Gettysburg, Then And Now: When and How the Regiments Fought and the Troops They Encountered.* Philadelphia: Gettysburg Battlefield Memorial Association, 1897. Reprint. Dayton, Ohio: Morninside, 1983.

Vaugh, Coleman. *Michigan Alphabetical Index Civil War 1861-1865.* Detroit: State Printer, 1915.

Walters, Sara. *Inscription At Gettysburg.* Gettysburg, Pennsylvania: Thomas, 1991.

Welcher, Frank J. *The Union Army 1861-1865: Organization and Operations.* Bloomington: Indiana University Press, 1989.

Zimmerman, Richard J. *Unit Organizations Of The Civil War.* Cambridge, Ontario: Rafm, 1982.

UNPUBLISHED SOURCES

Admission files to Michigan Old Soldiers' Home. State Library. Lansing, Michigan,

Bachelder, John B. Papers. New Hampshire Historical Society, Concord, New Hampshire.

Bancroft, John Milton. Journal. Michigan Historical Collection, University of Michigan. Ann Arbor, Michigan.

---. Papers. Edith Bancroft Collection. Bryn Athyn, Pennsylvania.

Barnes, Joel and Luke Barnes. Papers. Western Michigan University Library. Kalamazoo, Michigan.

Heckert Collection. Monroe County Historical Society. Monroe, Michigan.

Houghton, James. Journal. Michigan Historical Collection, University of Michigan. Ann Arbor, Michigan.

Jackson, W. H. Diary. Jean Denman Lavren Collection. Laurens, South Carolina.

Lamson, Alvan C. Letter. Michigan Historical Collection, University of Michigan. Ann Arbor, Michigan.

Pension Records, 4th Michigan Infantry. National Archives. Washington, D.C.

Seage, Henry. Journal. Steve Roberts Collection. Northville, Michigan.

Taylor, Edward Henry Courtney. Letters. Michigan Historical Collection. University of Michigan. Ann Arbor, Michigan.

United States Department of The Interior. Photographs. Gettysburg National Military Park. Gettysburg, Pennsylvania.

Vreeland, Michael. Papers and Photographs. U.S. Army Military History Institute. Carlisle Barracks, Carlisle, Pennsylvania.

---. Papers. Cecile Vreeland Collection. Waldport, Oregon.

NEWSPAPER SOURCES

Adrian Times Expositor. Adrian Public Library. Adrian, Michigan.

Cleveland Plain Dealer. Cleveland Public Library. Cleveland, Ohio.

Detroit Free Press. Wyandotte Library. Wyandotte, Michigan.

Grand Rapids Herald. Grand Rapids Public Library. Grand Rapids, Michigan.

Hillsdale Standard. Mitchell Public Library. Hillsdale, Michigan.
Hudson Gazette. Hudson Public Library. Hudson, Michigan.
Michigan Argus [Ann Arbor]. Dexter Historical Society. Dexter, Michigan.
Monroe Commercial. Monroe County Library. Monroe, Michigan.
Sturgis Journal. Sturgis Public Library. Sturgis, Michigan.
Toledo Blade. Toledo Public Library. Toledo, Ohio.

Index

[Note: Italizied page numbers indicate photographs]

Addison, Private 96, 97
Adrian, Michigan 15, 17, 19, 26, 28, 33, 41, 46, 60, 83, 85, 89, 98
Adrian College, Adrian, Michigan 20
Adrian Expositor 19
Aldie, Virginia 46, 47, 48, 49, 51, 52, 113
Alexandria Railroad 114
Ambulance Corps, Fifth 65
Anderson, Brig. Gen. George T. 65, 67, 71, 75
Andersonville Prison 94
Ann Arbor, Michigan 26, 112
Annapolis, Maryland 94
Antietam, Maryland 25, 84, 110, 111
Antietam Creek, Maryland 110, 111
Aquia Creek 37, 40
Arlington, Virginia 20
Army of Northern Virginia 36, 44, 50, 109
Army of the Potomac 20, 21, 44, 56, 57, 63, 113
Army of the Potomac, Second Corps 74, 75, 108, 111, 114
Army of the Potomac, Third Corps 47, 51, 63, 65, 66, 68, 69, 71, 74, 76, 110, 113
Army of the Potomac, Third Corps Hospital 103

Army of the Potomac, Fifth Corps 25, 29, 36, 37, 42, 47, 51, 53, 56, 59, 61-63, 65, 66, 68, 70, 72, 73, 79, 81, 108, 109-111, 113, 114
Army of the Potomac, Sixth Corps 111
Army of the Potomac, Eleventh Corps 47, 51, 108, 109
Army of the Potomac, Twelfth Corps 47, 50, 51, 63
Ashby Gap 45, 47, 49-51, 113
Augusta, Maine 119
Ayer, First Lt. Joseph C. 76

Baker, Pvt. John F. 90
Baker, Pvt. Moses 42
Baltimore, Maryland 111
Baltimore Pike 63
Bancroft, Lt. John M. 27, 28, 31, 33, 34, 37, 40, 43, 49, 51, 52, 54, 57, 61-64, 69, 71, 76, 80, 86, 88, 90, 99, 107, 110-113
Barbee's Cross-Roads 114
Barnes, Brig. Gen. James 25, 43, 49, 50, 69, 71-73, 76, 78, 105, 108
Barnes, Pvt. Luke 54
Barrett, Sgt. Orvey S. 34, 62, 71, 91, 95
Bauer, Pvt. Anton 95
Beal, Pvt. Henry 94

181

Bealeton, Virginia 92
Bealeton Station, Virginia 114
Beers, Second Lt. Jeptha 22
Bellows, Pvt. Alonzo 92
Benning, Brig. Gen. Henry L. 65, 73
Bensler, Pvt. Jacob 94
Beverly Ford 114
Billenger's Creek 54
Birney, Maj. Gen. David B. 64, 65
Blair, Gov. Austin 26, 29, 30, 111
Blankman, Pvt. George 18
Blue Ridge Mountains 34, 43
Boise, Pvt. Albert 97
Boonsborough, Maryland 109, 110
Bradford, Sgt. George W. 30
Brandy Station, Virginia 41
Brink, Pvt. James 99
Brinkerhoff Ridge 63
Bristoe Station 44
Brooke, Col. John 74, 75
Brownstown, Michigan 33
Bull Run 84
Burce, Pvt. Joseph 16, 46
Burke, Pvt. Eli 18
Burkettsville, Virginia 112
Burnside, Maj. Gen. Ambrose 39
Butterfield, Maj. Gen. Daniel 34, 47, 50

Caldwell, Brig. Gen. John 74, 76
Camp Williams 19, 26, 33
Campbell, First Lt. Robert 82, 84
Canada 16, 18
Carter Mill, Virginia 53
Catlett's Station, Virginia 44
Cemetery Ridge 63, 64, 74
Centreville, Virginia 45, 46, 52

Chamberlain, Surg. David P. 23
Chancellorsville 25, 29, 44, 84
Chandler, Zachariah 19
Chapin, Capt. Marshall W. 23
Chickahominy River 22
Childs, Maj. Jonathan W. 15, 23, 24
City Point, Virginia 24, 94
Cleveland, Ohio 20
Cleveland & Erie Railroad 20
Clymer, Doctor 39
Cooper, Pvt. William 94
Crawford, Pvt. Quimby Hugh 95
Creagerstown, Virginia 108
Cressey, Pvt. Noah 18
Cronenwill, Pvt. William 95
Cross, Col. Edward 74
Croswell, C. M. 19

Dates, Pvt. John J. 95
Dayton, Ohio 119
Dean, Sgt. John 54
Deardoff Farm 63
Deep Run Mill, Virginia 37
DePuy, First Lt. Richard B. 22
DeTrobriand, Col. Regis 64, 67, 71, 73-75
Detroit, Michigan 15, 26, 38, 39, 98
Detroit Free Press 15
Devil's Den 74
Dexter, Michigan 25, 26, 60, 112
Diffenbaugh, Drum Major Isaac 19
Dillion, Pvt. Beal 97
Divelbess, Pvt. George 92
Duffield, Lt. Col. William W. 15

Edwards Ferry, Virginia 53
Ellis's Ford 31

Emmitsburg, Maryland 108, 109
Emmitsburg Road 69
Ewell, Lt. Gen. Richard S. 50

Fairfax, Virginia 16, 46
Falmouth, Virginia 29, 38, 56
Fayetteville, Virginia 114
Field's Ford 40
Flera, Pvt. James C. 92, 94
Flowerfield, Michigan 18
Forbes, Pvt. Andrew 18
Fort Woodbury 20
Fountain, Pvt. Hiram 96, 97
Fox's Gap 112
Frederick, Maryland 54, 56, 58, 109
Fredericksburg, Virginia 25, 29, 30, 84, 92-94
Fredericksburg Road 40
French, Capt. Ebenezer 92, 93
Frizzellburg 57
Funkstown, Maryland 110

Gaines' Mill 22, 89
Georgetown, Pennsylvania 20
Georgia troops 75, 77
Georgia, 9th 77
Germantown, Pennsylvania 96
Gettysburg, Pennsylvania 14, 16, 22, 25, 30, 39, 44, 53, 58, 59, 61-64, 83, 85, 95, 98-101, 105, 107-112, 114, 115, 117, 118
Gettysburg Battlefield Commission 115
Gettysburg College, Gettysburg, Pennsylvania 52
Gilbert, Lt. Edwin 113
Goose Creek 53
Graham, Brig. Gen. Charles K. 64
Grand River, Michigan 119

Granger, Capt. David A. 16
Granite Schoolhouse 65
Gregery, Pvt. Charles W. 99
Gregg, Brig. Gen. David M. 36, 50
Griffin, Brig. Gen. Charles 21, 108, 111
Grove Church 40, 43
Gum Springs, Virginia 45-47, 51

Hall, Lt. Col. Jarius 24, 30, 80, *83*, 114
Hamp, Pvt. William 57
Hampton, Virginia 119
Hancock, Maj. Gen. Winfield Scott 74
Hanover Road 63
Hanover, Pennsylvania 59, 61
Harpers Ferry 25
Harrisburg, Pennsylvania 20
Hartwood Church 30
Heintzelman, Brig. Gen. Samuel P. 21
High Knob Pass 108, 109
Highland Avenue 63
Hill, Lt. Gen. A. P. 50
Hillsdale County, Michigan 18
Hillsdale Standard 44, 45
Hinchman, T. 113
Hooker, Maj. Gen. Joseph 34, 39, 45, 56
Houghton, Pvt. James 34, 40, 41, 43-45, 46, 48, 50, 58, 61, 62, 64, 69, 73, 76, 78, 86, 101, 102, 105
Houston, Texas 33, 85
Howard, Maj. Gen. Oliver O. 51, 108, 109
Hudler, Pvt. John 95
Hudson Gazette 96
Hudson, Michigan 31, 55
Humphreys, Maj. Gen. Andrew A. 110, 112

Indiana 16

Jackson, Sgt. William H. 45, 77
Jacksonville, Florida 94
Jacobs, Dr. Michael 52, 63, 64
Jeffords, Col. Harrison H. 22, 25, 26, 27, 29, 30, 59, *60*, 71, 77, 78, 80, 82, 83, 84, 86, 97, 105, 107, 112, 114-116
Jeffords, Solomon 25
Jeffords, Phebe 25
Johnson, Pvt. James 101, 102
Johnsville 57
Jones' Crossroads 110

Keedysville, Virginia 112
Kelly, Col. Patrick 74, 75, 77
Kelly's Ford 30-32, 34, 36, 37, 40, 42, 43
Kershaw, Brig. Gen. Joseph B. 73, 75, 78, 86
Kydd, First Sgt. John H. 77

LaGrange County, Indiana 16
Lake Michigan 94
Lee, Gen. Robert E. Lee 36, 39, 45, 47, 51
Leesburg, Virginia 47, 51, 53, 54
Leming, Musician Henry A. 18
Lenawee County, Michigan 18
Libby Prison 54
Liberty, Maryland 57
Lima, Michigan 25, 26, 112
Lincoln, Pres. Abraham 56, 60
Linden, Virginia 113
Little Ford 40-43
Longstreet, Lt. Gen. James 50, 51, 107
Loveland, Capt. William 113
Lovettsville, Virginia 113
Luce, Pvt. Moses A. 62

Lumbard, Col. George 22, 23, 24, 26, 27, 52, 78, 82, 86, 111
Lumbard, Lt. Horatio G. 43

Maine, 17th 64, 65, 69, 74, 76
Maltz, Second Lt. George L. 57
Malvern Hill 17, 18, 22, 23, 87, 89
Manassas 39, 44, 45, 51
Manassas Gap 113, 114
Manassas Junction 44
Manistee, Michigan 94
Marathon, Michigan 112
Marietta, Pennsylvania 99
Markham Station, Virginia 113
Marsh Creek 108
Martin, Pvt. Richard 18
Maryland 50, 58, 109
Mason-Dixon Line 59
Massachusetts 16, 25
Massachusetts, 3rd 49
Massachusetts, 5th 111
Massachusetts, 9th 20, 31, 63
Massachusetts, 11th 16
Massachusetts, 14th 20
Massachusetts, 32nd 31, 45, 46, 65, 67, 71, 76
Massachusetts Battery, 3rd 51, 86
McAllister Mill Road 65
McClellan, Maj. Gen. George 20, 21, 62
McDonough, Illinois 62
McLaws, Maj. Gen. Lafayette 50
McLean, Capt. James B. 40, 41, 42, 86, 102, 103, 105
McQuade, Col. James 25
McSherrytown Road 62
Meade, Maj. Gen. George G. 25, 37, 43, 47, 56, 57, 61-64, 56, 109

Mechanicsville 89
Michigan 15, 16, 20, 26, 30, 31, 37, 44, 76, 96, 99, 101, 111, 115, 119
Michigan, 5th 74, 76
Michigan, 11th 92
Michian Argus 114
Michigan troops 15, 16, 27, 29, 111
Middleburg, Virginia 47, 49, 51
Middletown, Maryland 108, 109
Miller, Pvt. John 16
Millerstown National Park 67
Milwaukee, Wisconsin 119
Miner, Pvt. Irwin 97
Miner's Hill, Virginia 21
Monocacy River 54, 56
Monroe, Michigan 23, 95
Monteith, Capt. George 113
Montreal 16, 18
Moon, John W. 56
Mooney, Pvt. John 16
Morell, Brig. Gen. George W. 21
Morgan, Pvt. Moses 99
Moritz Farm 108
Morrisville 43
Mosby, Maj. John S. 37, 47, 52, 113
Mountain Run 36
Mt. Pleasant 56

New York 96
New York, 25th 45
New York, 40th 64, 65
New York, 41st 20, 21
Newbridge, Virginia 21, 22
North Carolina Cavalry, 4th 41
Norton, Capt. Lemuel B. 113

Ohio 16

Orange & Alexandria Railroad 44

Paine, Capt. J. C. 113
Parker, Pvt. George 16
Partridge, Pvt. Larned 92
Patrick, Alexander D. 39
Peach Orchard 64, 67, 69
Pendleton, Pvt. James 99
Peninsula Campaign 21, 44, 84
Pennsylvania 45, 58, 59, 61, 86, 89
Pennsylvania, 62nd 25, 31, 39, 46, 67, 76, 77
Pennsylvania, 118th 67, 69
Pennsylvania, 155th 44, 61
Pennsylvania College 64
Pennsylvania Reserves 86, 102
Petersburg, Virginia 24, 31
Philadelphia, Pennsylvania 94
Pickett, Maj. Gen. George E. 50, 102
Piedmont, Virginia 113
Pipe Creek 57
Piper, Alanson R. 61
Pittsburgh, Pennsylvania 25
Pittsford, Michigan 97
Pleasonton, Maj. Gen. Alfred 47, 49, 50, 51
Plum Run 65, 77
Porter, Brig. Gen. Fitz John 21
Potomac Creek 29
Potomac River 54, 111
Preston, First Lt. Simon B. 22
Purcellville, Virginia 113
Purdy, Abe 112
Purdy, Pvt. George 99, 112

Quebec 18

Randolph, Capt. John M. 23
Rappahannock River 30, *32*, 34, 36, 41, 42, 114

Rectortown, Virginia 113
Regal, Pvt. Isaiah 90
Richmond, Virginia 94
Rickett, Sgt. Don 94
Robertson, Adj. Gen. Jonathan 15, 16, 37
Robinson, Capt. William F. 52, 63, 99
Rohrersville, Maryland 110
Rose, Capt. A. Morell 22, 23
Rose's Woods 64, 65, 69, 73-75, 77, 101, 115
Round Tops 63, 65, 74, 76, 86, 94, 103, 105, 107
Roxbury Mills, Maryland 110

Salsbury, Sgt. Lester H. 91, 92, 115
Schutze, Pvt. Charles 18
Seage, Chaplain John B. 31, 36, 37, 38, 39, 40, 55, 87, 91
Seage, Cpl. Henry 27, 31, 33, 40, 52, 54, *55*, 56, 57, 61, 78, 82, 101, 107, 108, 110, 111
Seage, Lt. R. Watson 29, 31, 30, 36, 57, 80, 87, 101, *104*, 107, 111, 115, 117
Sedgwick, General 110
Seitz, Lt. John 77, 78
Semmes, Brig. Gen. Paul 75, 77
Seven Days 84, 89
Sharpsburg 110
Sharpsburg Pike 111
Sherman, Brig. Gen. William T. 20, 21
Shiawassee Township 102
Sickles, Maj. Gen. Daniel E. 63, 64, 73
Slocum, Maj. Gen. Henry 50, 61
Slocum, Capt. Jeremiah D. 16
Smith, Pvt. Jackson 54
Smith, Gen. William F. 109

Snicker's Gap 50
South Carolina, 5th 75
South Carolina troops 73, 75, 77
South Mountain 109
Spencer, Musician LeRoy M. 18
Spotsylvania 92
Springfield Rifle 53, 63
St. Joseph County, Michigan 93
Steuben County, Indiana 16, 92
Stoneman's Switch 29
Stony Hill 64, 65, 67, 69, 71, 73, 75, 76, 78, 96, 115
Stuart, Maj. Gen. J.E.B. 50, 57
Summit House Hospital 94
Sweitzer, Col. Jacob Bowman 25, 36, 65, 67, 71, 74, 76, 77, 79, 81, 86, 89
Sykes, Maj. Gen. George 56, 57, 63-65, 69, 110-112, 114

Taneytown Road 65
Tarnsney, Color Bearer Thomas 80
Taylor, Cpl. Edward 29, 33, 42, 43, 90, 91, 96, 108, 109
Thoroughfare Gap 44
Thurston, Pvt. Epaminondas 94
Tilton, Col. William S. 65, 69, 71
Toledo, Ohio 20
Tolford, Pvt. William H. 96, 97, 99
Townsend, Adj. Gen. E. D. 56
Tracey, Pvt. George 102
Train, Pvt. Henry 56
Trostle's Woods 71, 74, 75, 95

U.S. Ford 42
Union Bridge 57

Union Mills, Maryland 57-59, 61, 62
Union, Virginia 113
Uniontown, Maryland 57
Unionville, Maryland 57, 58
United States Artillery, 2nd 21
United States Cavalry, 2nd 21
United States Volunteers 83, 85, 87
University of Michigan, Ann Arbor, Michigan 26
Upperville, Virginia 49
Utica, Virginia 108

Vanzile, Pvt. Riley E. 54
Vincent, Col. Strong 49, 51, 69
Virginia 16, 31, 36, 37, 45, 50, 51, 97, 108, 111, 113
Von Olker, Drum Major John 20
Vreeland, First Lt. Michael 31, 33, 80, 82, *85*, 99, 100, 108
Vreeland, William J. 33

Walcott, First Lt. Aaron F. 86
Walker, Pvt. George 57
Walker, Pvt. Samuel 99
Waller, Pvt. Francis 57
Ward, Brig. Gen. J. H. Hobart 64
Warren, Brig. Gen. Governeur K. 65, 109
Warrenton Branch Railroad 114
Warrenton Post Road 30
Warrenton, Virginia 113
Washington, D.C. 16, 19, 24, 37, 39, 44, 52, 54

Washington City, Maryland 20
Washtenaw County, Michigan 83
Watts, Surg. J. S. 91
Wayne County, Michigan 18, 28
Webster, Pvt. Noah 97
Weikert Farm 88, 107
West Point Academy 25
Westfall, Second Lt. Benjamin 96, 97, 98
Westfall, Pvt. Charles 96
Wheatfield 14, 24, 46, 64-68, 70, 72-79, 81, 86, 88-92, 95, 96, 98, 100-102, 104, 107, 109, 115
Wheatfield Road 65, 67, 69, 71, 74, 75
Wheaton, Pvt. Andrew 92
White Oak Swamp 89
White Pigeon, Michigan 38
Wilcox, Mrs. W. S. 19
Wilderness Campaign 22
Williamsport 111
Wilson, Pvt. Charles 99
Winchester Turnpike 47
Winslow, Capt. George B. 69
Wofford, Brig. Gen. William T. 75, 77
Wolf's Hill 63
Wood, Capt. Abram R. 21, 22
Woodbury, Col. Dwight A. 15, 16, *17*, 19, 22, 23, 24, 60

York, Pennsylvania 95

Zook, Brig. Gen. Samuel 74-77